GOING
FORWARD

GOING
FORWARD

A Life With Horses

JENNIE LORISTON-CLARKE
with Carolyn Henderson

Drawings by the late Anne Bullen

J A Allen

ISBN 0 85131 790 1
J.A. Allen
Clerkenwell House
Clerkenwell Green
London EC1R 0HT

J.A. Allen is an imprint of Robert Hale Ltd

British Library Cataloguing in Publication Data
A catalogue record for this book is available from the British Library

Design by Judy Linard
Edited by John Beaton
Printed by St Edmundsbury Press Limited, Bury St Edmunds
and bound by Woolnough Bookbinding Limited, Irthlingborough.

Acknowledgements

Thanks to Arnold Garvey, editor of *Horse & Hound*, for making archive issues available for research. Quotations are reproduced by permission.

Anne Bullen's drawings are reproduced from cards supplied by Gill Bullen and photographs are reproduced by permission of the copyright owners. In a few instances it has not been possible to trace the copyright owner and it is hoped that any such omission will be excused.

This book is dedicated to all those who have supported me, worked for me and enjoyed the lovely horses we have been lucky enough to train, and who have become our friends. It is also dedicated to my family – my daughters Anne and Lizzie, my brothers and sisters and my husband, Anthony, who has done so much to make our homes such lovely places in which we have enjoyed so much.

Jennie Loriston-Clarke

Contents

1

A Remarkable Family

Mention the name Jennie Loriston-Clarke to anyone remotely interested in horses and you will get instant recognition and reaction. As one of her pupils puts it: if she was a footballer, she would be a marketing man's dream – talent, determination that can harden into quiet but definite resilience and integrity in one package, minus any inconvenient dark secrets or skeletons in the closet.

The media calls her the doyenne of British dressage and describes her as one of the most vital influences there have ever been on the future of international breeding and production of competition horses. Her friends speak of her in glowing epithets, then, realising that they are making her sound like a saint on horseback, hurry to reassure you that she's straight as a die, extremely funny and the original soft centre… and yes, she can be terrifying if she wants to be, but it's only to make an eighteen-year-old would-be dressage star with a head too big for his riding hat realise that he's got at least another thirty years of hard work before he stands a chance of being as good as he thinks he is.

The trouble about being a living legend – another of the oft-used labels that make her wince – is that people tend to think that all the glory and success has happened as if by magic. The reality is that Jennie's success has come through hard work and tenacity, often in the face of difficulties that would have prompted many people to find an easier option or settle for second best. She comes from what is undoubtedly an extraordinary family with an equally extraordinary width and breadth of talent, but silver spoons have been in short supply. At times, her life so far has seemed to veer between extreme highs and lows like a roller coaster, but giving up is not in her vocabulary and never has been.

It is a life that has been centred around horses right from the start, thanks to her parents. Jennie was born in 1943, one of six children whose closeness has remained throughout childhood into their adult lives. Her father was Jack Fitzherbert Symes Bullen, a quiet man on whom the experiences of war must have had a profound effect. A gunner in the Royal Artillery, he fought at the Battle of the Somme and, at the age of seventeen, was the only boy from his school year to come home alive from that hellhole of mud, misery and appalling military strategy. In the Second World War, he was wounded but never spoke of his experiences: all he ever let slip was that his first job was to go out at the end of each day and shoot the wounded horses that would not survive.

War had a profound effect on his family in a way that those of the next generations can hardly comprehend. Before hostilities broke out, Jack and his brother, Henry, travelled round the world to study farming. They went first to Australia to study sheep farming, then to America where they trained horses and became real-life cowboys. When war started, Jack came home to fight but Henry felt differently and became a conscientious objector – a move which split the family irrevocably, as Henry was written off by his father and spent the rest of his life in America until his death about ten years ago.

Jennie remembers her father, who was invariably known as 'the Colonel,' as being very quiet, with the natural gift of winning respect from those who knew him. He never needed to raise his voice, with either people or animals, and if he gave an order, in his quiet way, it never crossed the recipient's mind to refuse it or question him. A tall, slim, good looking man, he could ride anything without resorting to force and would sit like glue to buckers that had learned to throw previous would-be riders. If a horse fell over, or laid down in a last ditch attempt to thwart its rider, Colonel Bullen would sit quietly but immovably until it realised that his way was the easiest.

That gift of inspiring others, which undoubtedly helped those who served under him in the Second World War, led to one of many hair-raising experiences in Jennie's childhood. A four-year-old pony called Star of Bethlehem somehow managed to fall down a cliff and cheated death by landing on a ledge halfway down, where it stood shaking in confusion and shock. The first attempt at rescuing it, by fastening ropes round its belly and lifting it with a tractor, had to be aborted when it became clear that there was a risk that the ropes were going to break. The only answer, decided Colonel Bullen, was to turn it round on the ledge and persuade it to jump into the sea.

Jennie, then aged twelve, was lowered on to the ledge beside the bewildered pony, where she was able to make sure that it was unhurt and – considering the predicament it had landed itself in – relatively calm. However, Star was not to be persuaded to jump out into space alone, so Jennie was instructed to blindfold him and turn him round. She then vaulted on to his back and, following her father's instructions, kicked the pony forwards over the edge and whipped off the blindfold as they went over, clinging onto its bare back. The water broke their fall and she was able to steer the pony back to shore with no harm to either of them.

It sounds – and was – like a scene from a film. But whereas the latter would involve a trained stuntman and equally highly trained horse, this rescue operation relied purely on a little girl's courage and implicit faith in her father. Jennie says, with absolute sincerity, that she never questioned anything he asked her to do because if he wanted her to do it, she knew she could.

Anne Bullen, Jennie's mother, was born Anne Harris St John and one of her ancestors was reputedly Master of the Horse to William the Conqueror – so if ability with and affinity for horses is innate, the family has far-reaching credentials. She was an immensely talented artist who could capture a horse or pony's character and movement: just by looking at her paintings, you can see that she had that mysterious 'eye for a horse' that can to a certain extent be learned through years of assessing animals, but also seems in rare cases to be an instinctive ability to look at a horse in rough or poor condition and see how it could look with correct care and schooling.

Not only was she ahead of her time in her requirements as to how a horse should go, she combined practical knowledge with an artist's eye and imagination. She could see something pulling a cart and turn it into a star, and frequently did just that. On one occasion, through a dealer called Mr Moss, she bought a 13.2hh grey pony who had once pulled a knacker's cart. She renamed him Silver Moon, though he was always known at home as Mossy, after the dealer who brought them together.

Mossy's real life story would almost have equalled that of the fictional Black Beauty. His original saviour, an Irish dealer, first saw him trotting down the street in Limerick, pulling a knacker's cart with a pathetic collection of old, worn-out animals tied behind it on their last journey back to the slaughterhouse. The Irishman spotted that there was a touch of quality about the pony, even though he was hatrack thin, and followed the cart back.

By the time they arrived it was dark, so he looked him over in the headlights of his car. Whether he recognised the hidden quality, felt sorry for the six-year-old whose emaciation and hanging head made him look much older or whether commercial sense and compassion became mixed Jennie never really found out, but he haggled the price until both were satisfied and set Mossy on the road to success. One thing that is certain is that if he had not seen him, the little grey would have been hammered round the roads until he was worn out and then he, too, would have met the same fate as the animals he was driven to collect.

Mr Moss tried to ship the pony over to England straight away, but he was so thin that the shippers refused to take him and the dealer had to spend three weeks getting some weight on him before he was judged fit to travel. Jennie recalls that judging by his state when he arrived, he must have been a walking skeleton when Mr Moss first saw him. She had never seen such a thin pony and once he had been wormed – undoubtedly the first time this had ever been done – her parents decided that the only way to improve his condition was to give him five small meals a day. Mossy must have thought he was in heaven, particularly when eggs and brandy were added to his food to build him up.

Although he was beautifully made and had lovely paces, which luckily had not been ruined by hammering round the streets pulling a cart, Mossy was the rawest of raw material. He could not canter, because he had been driven at either a fast trot or allowed to pace: a running gait where the horse's legs move in lateral rather than diagonal pairs. It took hours of patient work to teach him to go correctly, first on the lunge without the complication of a rider's weight and then, as he became stronger and better balanced, under saddle.

Mossy repaid the work many times over. He became a prolific winner in the show ring and earned a special place in Jennie's heart, not just for his ability but for the way his intelligence made him a joy to train and ride. He would come when she called him and was ready to have a go at anything, whether it was playing cowboys and Indians or jumping cross-country. After the Bullen children had years of fun with him, he lived long enough to teach Jennie's eldest daughter, Anne, to ride. Today he is immortalised in oils on Jennie's wall, his mane and tail blowing in the wind as he stands in perpetual freedom.

Anne Bullen's talent as an artist was as natural as her talent with horses. At the age of fourteen, she won a prestigious gold medal; that drawing, its lines filled with a flowing confidence far beyond its artist's years, is part of Jennie's precious collection. She studied in Florence and was equally happy working in pencil, watercolours or oils; she quickly became renowned for her ability to portray animals 'inside and out' and was often commissioned to produce portraits of horses and ponies, both competition stars and family favourites. On one occasion she managed a spectacular double deal, when the Maharajah of Jaipur bought a pony called Phantom and at the same time, commissioned a portrait of his son with it.

When you look at Anne Bullen's works, which have a timeless beauty half a century on, there is a sense that she knew just how a horse moved. When lesser artists paint a standing horse it often seems as if the vital spark which makes it a living, volatile animal has been frozen in the portrait, but when a work has her signature in the corner it is as if, like the one of Mossy, the pony is alert and ready to move at the slightest provocation. There are many examples in Anne Bullen's book, *Ponycraft* (Blandford Press 1956), and anyone lucky enough to find a copy should prize it for its simple, common sense advice and delicate, detailed illustrations.

The first family home, the original Catherston Stud, was set in the Dorset hills overlooking the sea and the village of Charmouth and had been owned by the Bullen family for many years. The estate covered 2000 acres and incorporated five farms, including a big dairy farm. A photograph of the house itself shows it as attractive and impressive but somehow slightly intimidating; the end walls are covered in ivy and the inhabitants, presumably both family and people from the estate, are posed in the formal manner of the time. Or perhaps it just gains that intimidating shadow when you learn of its history – Judge Jeffreys, the infamous 'hanging judge' stayed there and nearly fell foul of a plot to murder him. Considering the number of lives he ended at the gallows and the fear and hatred he inspired, it is perhaps surprising that the attempt failed. A mounting block carved with the date, some time in the seventeenth century, recorded the event, though neither Jennie nor her brothers and sisters realised that every time they got on a pony, they were standing on a piece of history.

Jennie, who is not given to flights of fancy, believes that one room was haunted. The family often heard people banging on the doors, but when this was investigated no one was ever there. Even though she was sure that the ghosts were friendly, she was always careful to shut every door behind her as she walked through the house in case someone - or something – was following.

Once inside the imposing front door, a small flight of stairs led to a landing dominated by a stained glass window that would be the envy of owners of many country houses today. The stairs continued to the upper floors, which had oak-panelled galleries running all the way round. Most of the house was Elizabethan, with eighteenth century additions made by Jennie's great grandfather. It had its own churchyard in which members of the family were buried... so perhaps those unseen presences were benevolent ancestors.

The Bullens' marriage was, it seems, a strong and happy one even if life was not easy. Living in the manor house and controlling the estate was not a matter simply of dispensing largesse, it was a gruelling responsibility. Jennie was aware, even as a little girl and with parents determined to do the best to provide a happy childhood, that her father was not well and that the almost intolerable burden of running such a huge estate was not helped by others who were less honourable. She and her siblings also learned to treat others with courtesy and respect, whether they were visitors or people who worked for the estate.

This came not so much through conscious 'social training' as from an acceptance that this was the way you should behave and is a legacy which has remained with Jennie throughout her life. Anyone meeting her for the first time is always amazed how approachable she is, little realising that even now, the worse possible ordeal for her is to enter a roomful of strangers. Yet at the same time, she can be a consummate entertainer, holding huge audiences spellbound at lecture demonstrations.

Adopting another persona – the public Jennie – is her way of coping with a lifetime of shyness. It is also just one example of the way she has learned to use lateral thinking to solve whatever difficulties are thrown at her, whether it is a horse which finds it difficult to perform a particular movement or a staff logistics problem. In all walks of life, you find some people who say 'I can't do this' and others who say 'I can't do this in the obvious way, so I'll have to find another one.' Jennie definitely falls into the latter category, which may be an attitude learned unconsciously from her mother.

For a lot of the time, Mrs Bullen was responsible for running Catherston – particularly the horse side, which was important as horses were not only an enjoyable part of life, they also paid the bills. With six children – Anthony, who was only sixty when he died, Michael, Charlie, Jennie, Jane and Sarah – plus the horses and her painting, life must have been full to the brim. That again is an example Jennie follows: she may have officially retired from top class competition riding, but at half past eight she is likely to have already ridden two horses before a day crammed full with teaching, judging and running the stud. Even at the end of the day, the phone hardly seems to stop and in the stud season, there will be mares due to foal that need to be checked.

Even when Jennie was a child, horses had to pay their way – and often pay for many other things, too. The original Catherston was so huge it cost a small fortune just in fuel and electricity; Jennie remembers that they had to make £1800 a year before they could even live there, which in those days was a considerable sum. The final straw came when the water pipes to the house and surrounding district had to be replaced, the cost of which fell to the Bullens.

Horses therefore had to subsidise the farming. This gave Mrs Bullen the chance to make the most of her ability not only to spot potential, but to produce it, sometimes in almost unbelievable ways. She loved nothing better than to buy a shaggy pony and work her magic on its appearance and performance. On one occasion, she excelled herself: a wealthy lady wanted a show pony that would go to Harringay, then the Mecca of the showing world, and came to see a nice moving grey that had just started its schooling. The asking price was £500, but it wasn't good enough. The lady wanted, in her own words, 'a thousand pound pony.'

Without missing a beat, Mrs Bullen told her that although this pony was nice, she had an absolutely spectacular one arriving soon that would be ready for sale in about three weeks. After extracting a promise that no one else would be allowed to look at it before she had been given the chance to do so, the lady left, undoubtedly dreaming of the championship rosettes and silver trophies to come.

Next day, Mrs Bullen clipped the pony out completely to enhance its beautiful conformation – which she had spotted in the rough – gave it a little more food to give it show ring condition and started a three-

Dartmoor Ponies

week schooling regime. At the end of the schooling period, she rang up the would-be winning owner and promised her that she had just the pony she was looking for. Eagerly her customer returned, saw the pony, and – not realising she had earlier rejected it as not up to top class competitions – happily handed over twice the original asking price.

The Bullens also ran riding courses for children, and these proved so essential to the family economy that they were known as the 'heating and lighting courses,' because this was what they paid for. About twenty-five children at a time would descend on Catherston, which was great fun for the Bullen children but must have been a Herculean task for their parents and for Greta Phillips, a family friend who helped with the teaching. Many famous names can count a heating and lighting course as their induction into the basics of riding and horsemanship, including the now Captain Mark Phillips, a top international event trainer and course designer who won many top titles during his riding career.

As a useful offshoot to the riding courses, Mrs Bullen would buy unhandled, unbroken ponies off the Welsh hills. Under her supervision, her children would then back them and get them going so that they were safe for youngsters to ride, handle and have fun with, and then at the end of the courses the ponies would often be sold to the pupils' satisfied parents.

Fifty years on, the Bullens' childhood sounds as if it was a magical experience. In many ways it was, but it was perhaps unusual even then. The differences in their ages meant that they naturally fell into pairs; Michael and Anthony were the oldest and were at school, whilst Jane and Sarah, the youngest two, made another natural pair. That left Jennie and Charlie, who were eighteen months apart and spent most of their time in each other's company.

Charlie was the original wild child, always tearing about and getting into everything. A sort of Just William with brains and charm, he had a knack for getting himself into trouble but an equal talent for extricating himself. Occasionally, even he had to admit that what started off as – in his view – a good way of having fun was not the success he had imagined.

Jennie recalls one particular occasion when their father was away and

Charlie managed to find the key to the gun cabinet. At first intending to just take out and admire a rifle, he was unable to resist the temptation when he realised the cartridges were also there. Dismissing Jennie's doubts as to whether this was actually a good idea, he persuaded her that the house's long passage made a perfect shooting gallery, and was doing quite well with his target practice until the gun jammed.

Using all his charm, Charlie persuaded one of the farmhands to sort it out and he and Jennie then went off to try and shoot crows. When they had finished, Charlie returned the gun to the cabinet and locked it up in the assumption that no one would be any the wiser. Unfortunately for him, next time Colonel Bullen went to the cabinet he realised it had been tampered with and demanded to know who was responsible. Charlie owned up immediately and was soundly whacked.

As children, Jennie and Charlie were total opposites, which may account for why they got on so well together. Her recollection, which is probably rather harsh, is that she was very wet and feeble, so much so that she recalls she had the nickname Feeble Fanny. She says she was always falling down and hurting herself, and was the perfect victim for the unmalicious but tough Charlie. One of his favourite tricks was to tie her to the chair by her hair; in this double act, Charlie was the ringleader and Jennie the stooge, but although he was a little tyrant within the family circle, he would have given his all to protect her from any outside threat.

Catherston had its own woods, which became another world for the Bullen children. They had a freedom that today's children can only imagine; the Bullens knew that they had nothing to fear except their children's sense of adventure. Having said that, some of their escapades – such as midnight feasts of chestnuts roasted on fires struck from flints – were arranged without parental knowledge. These involved leaving via the bedroom windows, then running along a narrow wall across a pole thirteen feet from the ground. It was quite a feat for a 'Feeble Fanny,' but Jenny admits that she only did it because Charlie told her to!

Jennie, Sarah and Jane – now Jane Holderness-Roddam and an equally influential figure in the horse world, particularly through her involvement with horse trials – have a close relationship. But at one stage, as so often happens, poor Jane and Sarah were the younger sisters who were just that little bit too young to be treated as equals. Though they tried desperately to keep up with their older siblings, the younger two sometimes ended up trailing in their wake.

In the single-minded way that children have, the older ones decided that this did not fit in with their plans. They had created homes in the woods complete with ovens – old biscuit tins dug into the banks underneath which fires could be set – and did not want Jane and Sarah interfering with them. To avoid this, they told them that the woods were full of lions and tigers, a ploy so successful that Jane and Sarah were terrified of being eaten by wild animals. This worked for several years, until the day Mrs Bullen was visited by Glenda Spooner, then a judge and later respected throughout the world as an authority on showing and a campaigner for equine welfare. As she approached the house, Mrs Spooner was met by Jane, who seriously confided the problems they had to cope with being surrounded by such wild and ferocious beasts. Mrs Spooner's first words to Mrs Bullen were of the nonsense she had filled her children's heads with, which did not go down too well.

Charlie's fearlessness often got him into scrapes, but one of his worst accidents happened when he was eight years old, after a momentary and almost lethal lapse of concentration. Always the sort of boy who enjoyed getting involved with farm and estate work, he was left in the charge of the bailiff whilst his parents went to a show. He went to open a gate, then walked back across the road – and somehow did not realise that a car was coming towards him and stepped straight in front of it. The driver swerved, but could not avoid him and sent Charlie hurtling to the side.

That brief impact nearly severed his right arm. He was rushed to Exeter Hospital, where surgeons carried out a complicated tendon transplant operation as his parents travelled back through the night. The injury was so serious that Charlie spent much of the next two years in hospital, visited frequently by his brothers and sisters. He had to endure many tendon transplants to try and restore the arm's mobility, though his ebullient personality helped him bounce back when less courageous children would have given up. When he came out of hospital, he had to wear a sling and a cradle device on his hand and was encouraged to ride, as holding the reins helped to restore his arm function. Today, the only legacy of his accident is that he cannot move his right hand from side to side, though he can lift his arm and use his fingers.

The accident meant that his partnership with Jennie became even closer, as the time in hospital interfered so much with his schooling that it was decided he would join in with the girls' lessons at home. Mrs Bullen did not believe that girls should go to school, so they were educated at home and became even more reliant on each other for company and fun. Their life was a mixture of the relaxed and the regimented: the children's old nanny, Nicey Dangerfield, tried to keep track of their exploits if their mother was away and Greta Phillips was another favourite.

Later, Jennie realised that the closeness of the Bullen family perhaps helped Mrs Phillips survive the tragedies of her own life. Her daughter, Felicity, was killed in a terrible riding accident and when Jennie was about ten years old, Mrs Phillips gave her Felicity's riding clothes. Six months after Felicity's death, she lost her husband in the desert war; in the unconditional way that children have, the young Bullens gave her their affection and support just as their parents did all they could to help.

Formal lessons were the province of Mr Pulpher, a retired school-master who taught them the basics of reading, writing and numeracy. Although she was an intelligent child with natural common sense, Jennie found learning to read quite hard and remembers that because Mr Pulpher used a little book with nursery rhymes and illustrations, she learned to match up the words to the pictures and learn them by heart rather than reading them. Much later on in life, she realised that she was dyslexic, a condition that is well recognised today and which is connected with eye movement. The only way Jennie can describe the condition, which causes her few problems today, is that she has to focus on written words in a circular rather than linear direction.

This technique, which she developed through trial, error and a characteristic refusal not to give in, made it easier for her to learn and read French and Latin. Her determination was given another boost when Greta Phillips gave her a book called *The Montana Adventure*, about her uncle, Henry, and his adventures in America. She was so keen to read it that she spent hours practising the techniques which worked for French and Latin and applying them to English, and by the time she was about fourteen had conquered her reading difficulties.

Jennie's determination also helped to at least partly mend a family rift. She was so fascinated by the exploits of Uncle Henry that she wanted to find out more about him, and her father suggested that she wrote to him. Although it took a lot of concentration and effort, Jennie did just that and was thrilled to get a letter in reply, together with a photograph of her uncle. Michael later went out to America to meet him, though Jennie never managed to do so.

Jock Smith, who had been their father's batman, was another important influence because it was he who was responsible for their very first riding lessons. Jennie started riding at the age of three on a Dartmoor pony called Darkie, who her mother taught to perform a variety of tricks, so she really did grow up on horseback. As a tiny tot, she could do little except enjoy herself and develop the all-important sense of balance and security that few children today are given the chance or even permitted to acquire. Later, she graduated to Foxy, who taught the whole family to ride but was very difficult to catch. If he saw Jennie approaching with a headcollar, he would show a turn of speed that he never deployed when ridden, and gave her the first essential lessons in outwitting a devious pony. Later still came a pony called Kangaroo, who looked like a barrel on legs but became one of her favourites.

Jock, who was so fat that he waddled as he walked, was a kind and gentle man who thought the world of his charges. He took them out on their ponies and helped instil the basics. To this day, Jennie remembers the rhyme he taught them: 'Keep your head and your heart well up, Your hands and your heels well down, Your legs close to your horse's side, Your elbows close to your own.'

The important thing about those lessons, and with later ones when Mrs Bullen stepped in to polish their technique, was that they were fun. The children were just as happy riding bareback as on saddles and their little outdoor schooling area, formerly a tennis court, was just as likely to be used as an impromptu circus ring. They would slide off their ponies' tails, pretend to be cowboys and Indians and emulate the rosinback riders of the circus ring who balanced, standing, on their horses' broad backs. Today, Health and Safety laws mean that any riding school which encouraged such activities – even though the children always wore hats and safe footwear – would be closed down. But as Jennie points out, it made them agile and athletic and taught them how to be at one with their ponies.

They grew up not only in the countryside, but as a part of it. They were aware without being formally taught of the need for looking after their environment and protecting and controlling wildlife. Hunting, now such a controversial issue, was an accepted and necessary part of life; if you did not keep down the number of foxes by what true country people believed (and still do) was the most humane method, you lost the home-produced chickens, ducks and geese that helped keep you self-sufficient and well fed. Hunting was a natural part of life, and the children were also allowed to help with the hounds. Far from turning them into the heartless little monsters of animal rights propaganda, it made them even more aware of their responsibilities towards the countryside in general and animals in particular.

Hunter trials, cross-country competitions over natural fences designed to test horse and rider's courage and athleticism, provided enormous entertainment. The Bullens had a family team comprising Colonel and Mrs Bullen on their hunters, Mary Mitchell, the Colonel's secretary and Jennie. Jennie rode the team's secret weapon, an Exmoor pony called Skipper who had been bought for £15 off the moor and was first ridden by Mike and Charlie. He was a wonderful jumper but had absolutely no brakes in the conventional sense. Jennie soon learned, though, that an unconventional approach worked wonders. If she kept hold of the reins, Skipper would gallop all day and jump anything; if she wanted to stop, she had to turn him off his track and drop the reins. Mary, who later married and became Mary Robertson, was an important member of the team and the household and remained a close friend; she still lives on the same farm and she and Jennie caught up with their news only recently at a golden wedding celebration.

At one competition, the pair jumped a four foot nine fence with a five foot spread and their jumping prowess became so legendary in local circles that bets were laid on whether or not the pony could jump an enormous hedge. He did, Jennie giving a lead to her parents without realising that the cheers which went up as they landed were at least partly due to those who had faith in her ability putting their money where their convictions lay!

Although the Bullen children probably learned more through their everyday lives and responsibilities than could ever have been instilled in a classroom, the girls' conventional education had to progress. Charlie, who by then had come to the end of a long series of operations on his arm, went back to school and a qualified and seemingly charming governess was appointed to take charge of Jane, the then eleven-year-old Jennie and Sarah. It was the start of a horrifying episode that blighted Jennie's life and which she will never forget.

She now realises that the young Irish woman who arrived to teach them with such impeccable references was mentally ill, but all she knew at the time was that they were caught in an unpredictable and terrifying cycle of violence. To children who had been brought up to respect their elders, to know the difference between right and wrong and to accept that misdemeanours must be paid for, it was as bewildering as it was frightening. The Bullen children were certainly not saints – they were too high spirited and adventurous for that – but neither were they sinners.

As soon as lessons with the new governess began, they realised that she was a Jekyll and Hyde character. One minute she was patient and ready to explain anything they did not understand, but the next she would be bitingly sarcastic if any of her pupils made a mistake. This was an attitude the children could not understand, as their parents had always told them that the only things that mattered were that they worked hard, did their best and behaved responsibly towards others. Colonel and Mrs Bullen were strict – and it was accepted on both sides that if you were irresponsible or rude to people who were not in a position to answer back, such as members of staff, you ran the risk of a parental slap.

However, the new governess was far more than strict and anyone who behaved today as she did then would be convicted of child abuse. If any of the children failed to understand her, or behaved in a way that she felt slighted her authority, she made them kneel in front of her and hold out their hands. Then, telling them quite calmly that this was what Jesus had to endure, she beat them with a driving whip.

What made the girls even more bewildered was that seconds later, the pleasant side of her personality would surface and she would take them for nature study walks. Not surprisingly, they grew to dread their lessons, especially as the torments became more refined. Once they were given twenty minutes to learn twenty lines of poetry, and when their time was up, the slightest mistake was the prompt for a beating.

This went on for three years, with Colonel and Mrs Bullen totally unaware of what was happening behind the schoolroom door. Parents of modern children and even the children themselves will wonder how such confident and self-sufficient youngsters could stay quiet in the face of such treatment, but you have to remember that this was the first time in their lives that they had been treated anything other than fairly. Because they had been brought up to respect adults in positions of authority, they felt that they were in the wrong, even if they could not understand why.

The atmosphere and tension between governess and pupils built up like a storm waiting to break, and when it did break, it was in spectacular fashion. Jennie took her own 'punishments' in stoic fashion, but when the governess took her whip to Sarah, the baby of the family, she could take no more. Her anger gave her strength and she turned on the governess almost before the woman realised what was coming. In a swift sequence of actions, Jennie pushed her round, twisted her arm behind her back and thrust her head through the window so she was hanging half out of it with her legs dangling off the ground.

At the same time, she shouted to Jane to go and fetch her mother. When the horrified Mrs Bullen came running up to the schoolroom, the children poured out the saga of the past three unhappy, violent years with the result that the governess was sacked on the spot. She had, before coming to the Bullens, been governess to some very influential people. How many other children's lives had been marred by her unpredictable violence can only be wondered at, but what really surprised and revolted Jennie was that many years later, when the announcement was made of her marriage to Anthony, the Irish governess wrote to her offering congratulations as if nothing had ever happened. The letter, but not the memories, went straight in the bin.

2

'Ask a Mare'

Riding and competing the family ponies also had a serious side, in that competition successes acted as advertisements and drew potential customers to Catherston. Jennie and Jane inevitably stood top of the line on the family's show ponies, which was a little demoralising for other competitors. However, the atmosphere was mainly one of amicable competition, with just the occasional rival who was less than friendly. Above all, it was fun – these ponies were not wrapped up in cotton wool and treated as if they were china ornaments, they were all-rounders who could and did have a go at anything and just happened to be superb show ponies as well.

Many of today's parents and producers who talk in terms of five-figure sums for top class showing stars would be horrified to think of their investments going hunting and show jumping and joining in unofficial races. The ponies themselves would probably think it was a wonderful idea, far better than the restricted lifestyles many of them seem to lead. And as Jennie points out, a child's pony can have sparkle but it should still have manners – and how much better to teach it obedience and give it confidence by Mrs Bullen's methods than to tie its head down and lunge it for hours before it can be deemed safe for a child to get on.

Today, most riders assume that to produce a successful animal at top level for the show ring it is essential to have all mod cons, including a specially constructed manege and a luxury horsebox. There are a few who manage to do it on a shoestring, schooling their ponies in the field and travelling them to shows in trailers pulled by the family cars, but they are in the minority. Many of today's superstars are produced in professional yards and ridden by children who almost make a career out of it, so the genuinely family-owned and produced pony has to match up to those standards.

For Jennie and Jane, it was a very different story. They had a small schooling area, in reality the tennis court, but most of the schooling was done in the fields or out on rides. They learned to trot up and down hills, which was a wonderful way of building up the ponies' muscles and teaching them to balance themselves, and to extend and collect. Today, Jennie has a purpose-built indoor school and an international-sized outdoor manege, but her horses still hack out and are still schooled outside the confines of an arena.

One of the reasons for Anne Bullen's success was that she was ahead of her time. She had a clear understanding of dressage – which literally means 'training' – and of balance and collection. In the 1950s, dressage as a sport was only just beginning, but Jennie recalls that her mother taught her ponies to go in the same way as modern dressage horses are taught to go. She taught them exercises such as half pass, where the pony moves forwards and sideways at the same time, and shoulder-in, which helps develop balance and suppleness.

Shows were a huge adventure and although the family had a lorry, it was a very basic one with a canvas roof – a far cry from the houses on wheels that roll up to today's shows, complete with everything from showers and microwave ovens to luxurious sleeping accommodation. The Bullen girls camped out in their lorry with the ponies, and it was probably the ponies who had the best deal.

If a show was too far for the ancient lorry to reach, such as the Royal Highland Show in Edinburgh, the ponies would travel by train. They would board at Axminster, accompanied by one groom, and travel overnight. The family would meet them at the appropriate station and would then often ride them from there to the showground. There was, of course, much less traffic on the roads in those days, so they could be ridden to the showground in safety, but it all helped to accustom the ponies to a huge variety of sights, sounds and experiences.

Jumping was part of everyday riding and the family had some unlikely sounding stars. One mare, Polly Flinders, was bought as part of a batch to be schooled and sold but her departure was postponed when she got colic. After she recovered, Mrs Bullen told Jennie that she might as well have a bit of fun jumping her – something which the then twelve-year-old Jennie was full of enthusiasm for, as she had never had a jumping pony. The pair was entered for Richmond, with no one expecting spectacular results, but they proceeded to jump five feet out of a trot followed by five clear rounds one after another.

As this sort of talent was too good to ignore, the partnership of Polly Flinders and Jennie was entered at other shows during the year and they continued to bring home the rosettes. Curious as to where the little mare had inherited or aquired such ability, Mrs Bullen did some detective work and found that they were not the first people to have discovered it. The pony had come out of Ireland, where she had been jumped as a three and four-year-old and pushed too hard. As often happens when a youngster is put under too much pressure, Polly Flinders started to nap and was rejected and joined a boatload of dealers' horses bound for England.

Althought the Bullens were careful not to overjump her, a year later she again decided that she had had enough and would not jump in the ring – as soon as she heard the loudspeakers at a show, she would mentally shut off. Life as a Pony Club pony proved to be much more to Polly Flinders' taste than life as a pure show jumper, and she found so much new enthusiasm that she was sold to a girl rider to start competing in one-day events. Polly did a good job, because her new owner later became a member of the British eventing team in Kiev, where unfortunately she was one of many to suffer a crashing fall. All the Bullens' horses and ponies were individuals, not simply potential profits on four legs, and they kept in touch with Polly's progress, as they did with all their animals whenever possible. Polly was one of many whose lives remained linked with theirs, and at the end of her days she came back to them and found yet another new lease of life as a driving pony.

The philosophy of being responsible for the animals you breed and sell has been part of Jennie's life ever since. Catherston horses have always been in demand, both because of their breeding and also the good conformation, temperament and movement that usually go with it. With the youngsters that have been backed and ridden on, buyers also know that the vital early education that can have a permanent effect on a horse's future has been done properly. Jennie's philosophy is that doing everything you can to match the right horse with the right owner is in everyone's interest, even hers – the last thing she wants is for a Catherston horse to end up in an unsuitable home and perhaps gain an undeserved bad reputation.

Another jumping pony she remembers with affection is a 14.2hh mare called Storm III. Always turned out to perfection, thanks to Mrs Bullen's clever hand with the clippers, she was a great performer, though Jennie remembers her mother saying that if the mare was allowed to have hairy heels, she could be a carthorse instead of a show jumper. It was Storm who provided Jennie with a less than flattering press cutting, after a reporter covering a show for *Horse & Hound* wrote that 'the junior jumping was not of a very high standard, and was won by Jennie Bullen on Storm III'!

One of the orginal Catherston Stud's first well-known stallions was Bubbly, a stunning 13.2hh palomino, who was national palomino pony champion for ten years running and whose name lives on in the breeding of many of today's top class ponies. Photographs show him to be a perfect pattern of a riding pony, with a beautiful head and breath-taking colouring – he was a living example of the perfect palomino with a body the colour of a newly minted gold coin and a flowing white mane and tail. Apart from his physical beauty, he had a wonderful temperament which he passed on to his offspring and was beautifully behaved when ridden by Jennie or Jane. In those days, the idea of women – let alone girls – having anything to do with stallions was frowned on, as it was thought that only men should care for and handle them, but Bubbly set the practice of a lifetime for Jennie. Ever since, she has had the ability to build a rapport and mutual respect with stallions.

Bubbly lived with his mares and foals on Stonebarrow Hill, on grazing which dropped down to a cliff. One of Jennie's favourite jobs was to ride up on Mossy to check them, which she did by waiting at the fence which surrounded the sixty acres and giving a piercing whistle. As soon as he heard the sound Bubbly would round up his family and bring them galloping over. It was a sight Jennie will always treasure, the little gold stallion with the charisma that far outstripped his size bringing up to twenty-five mares and foals for inspection.

The ponies had the best of both worlds, enjoying the freedom to roam in their own little kingdom and to establish the natural hierarchies of the herd whilst being kept safe, healthy and in good condition by their owners. Every autumn, the herd would be brought back to their winter quarters at Catherston so that the foals could be weaned and the mares kept near the house to make it easier to feed them and keep an eye on them in the bad weather. This annual event had a magic of its own.

First Bubbly would be caught and tacked up, and it is further proof of his wonderful temperament that he accepted this as he accepted everything else. He and whoever was riding him would then drive the mares and foals home, heading off the hill down the A35 into Charmouth and then into Catherston Lane. It was like a Wild West stock drive – to keep the pony herd together, Jennie and her brothers and sisters had to canter them through and out of the sixty-acre field and then slow them right down to cope with a steep hill. They looked on bringing in the ponies as one of the highlights of their year.

Bubbly's stock was much sought after and succeeded in all disciplines, but one who did well in the show ring was actually an accident. Anthony Adverse, who proved to be a fabulous jumper and came fifth in the leading show jumper of the year competition at Harringay, was his first foal, born on the wrong side of the stable door after an illicit liaison with a pony mare. This was one of several surprisingly early encounters for Bubbly: he sired his first foals, including this one, as a yearling. His breeder, Mrs Franks, had not thought for a moment that he was old enough to have the inclination, let alone the ability, but he proved her wrong on both counts.

As Catherston ponies continued to chalk up an ever-increasing list of winnings, so the number of people who wanted to own one increased. In the mid-1950s an American pony enthusiast, Miss Alicia Stubbings, bought three ponies which had been virtually undefeated – the 12.2hh Coed Coch Pryderi, the hand bigger Criban Bumble and the 14.2hh Royal Show. They were all either first and champion or second in their classes at the Royal International Horse Show and Miss Stubbings, the niece of the American millionaire John Pierpoint Morgan, decided that she would take them home and show the American and Canadian showing fraternities what was being bred across the Atlantic.

Miss Stubbings was a dynamic and determined woman and when she decided something was going to happen, it did. Her enthusiasm for the Catherston ponies prompted an incredible three-week adventure for Jennie and Jane, because when she took her Royal International champions home she also took their jockeys on a Pan American jet to Washington. Even for today's sophisticated children, many of whom become used to flying abroad on holiday, travelling to the United States is in another league – but in those days, it was real pioneering stuff. As children, they rarely went out of the county apart from going to shows, and the only visit to London Jennie can recall was to see the coronation. What was just as if not more more exciting than the brief sight of their new queen was that the coronation gave them their first chance to see an event on television. Jennie recalls being taken to a house to watch the procession go past, then seeing the rest of the ceremony on television.

The Palomino

The flight to America had none of the luxury associated with modern air travel. From the children's point of view it centred on a lot of waiting about, though once the flight was underway they were invited to visit the flight deck. The ponies, in the care of Colonel and Mrs Bullen, adapted well to the experience of air travel. Later, the Colonel revealed that the worst experience had been when one of the flight crew asked him if he had a humane killer in case anything went wrong during the flight: he did not, and fortunately did not need one. Years later, there was an eerie echo of that incident when Sarah, who became an accomplished actress, won the role of one of the team members in the film *International Velvet*. Starring Tatum O'Neal as the spoilt brat who learns through her ambitions to become an Olympic event rider that horses are the ultimate levellers, it includes a heart-rending episode where one of the American team horses goes berserk on the transporter plane and has to be shot.

The cleverly named Prosperity of Catherston, who was out of a Connemara cross Arab mare called Fortune II, and one of many stunning ponies by Bubbly, was one of those who nearly went out to fly the flag. Bred by Mrs Thalia Gordon-Watson, mother of international event rider Mary, she was totally elegant, but with a refined substance that is so sought after but rarely seen. She won numerous championships and was nearly sold to America, but fortunately for Jennie, Miss Stubbings instead allowed them to keep her for breeding. Prosperity repaid this generous gesture many times over, producing a host of champions such as Catherston Safe Deposit, Catherston Nightsafe and Catherston Sunday Collection.

When the girls arrived in Washington with Miss Stubbings, they were treated with overwhelming friendliness. Their transatlantic showing debut, at Washington Show, did not go quite as they had hoped and for the first – and last – time, Catherston ponies stood at the bottom of the line. It was not that they were inferior to the American ponies, simply that the types and manner of presentation were worlds apart. The American ponies were 'gaited' and moved with a high-stepping action that to British and European eyes would be associated with a Hackney driving pony. They also had hogged (or roached, as the Americans term

Right: Jennie with her Mother

Below: Anne Bullen with her circus pony Darkie. Darkie raised hundreds of pounds for charity performing at shows around the country. Jennie learnt to ride on Darkie

Above: Jennie's father
and his family
outside the original
Catherston

Below: Uncle Henry
Bullen from the
photograph that he
sent Jennie

Opposite page top:
Jennie on Foxy, the
pony who taught all
the Bullen children
so much

Opposite page below:
Charlie and Jennie
with Mary Mitchell
at the Three
Counties Show

Jennie and Anne Bullen. Anne Bullen was a talented artist whose line drawings appear in this book

Above: (*centre*) Sarah on Silver Dollar and Jane on Ophelia at one of the 'light and heat' courses

Right: Skipper, an Exmoor pony, was one of the most successful cross-country ponies Jennie ever rode. He ended his days in a Devon pub where he was a firm favourite

Bubbly – for ten years he was champion palomino stallion

Right: Jennie dressed by her
mother in a bright green dress to
show off Bubbly; the judge was
suitably impressed and they won!

Below: Bubbly

A publicity photograph of Jennie (aged 12) and Jane (aged 7) on their arrival in New York (*Pan American World Airways*)

it) manes, clipped off completely down to the neck, and the muscles under the tops of their tails were nicked to give an artificially high carriage. When three ponies with plaited manes, natural tail carriage and extravagant but much lower action were introduced alongside them in the ring, the judges and spectators did not know what to make of them.

Realising that if she could not beat them, she somehow had to convert them, Miss Stubbings moved ponies and riders on to New York. After less than two hours' discussion she persuaded the show committee of the prestigious Madison Square Gardens Show to introduce a hunter pony division to the schedule. It was an enormous success, and Jennie and Jane found themselves with the winners' ribbons once again.

The same happened at the Royal Winter Fair in Toronto, and it says an enormous amount for the American and Canadian equestrian worlds' open mindedness that they took the girls, their ponies and all that they represented to their hearts. More than that, they enterered into these new divisions with the same enthusiasm they showed for their own. If the British government knew then what the pony world knows now, it would have given Miss Stubbings and the Bullen sisters an award for industry, because between them they started an enormously successful trade of riding ponies to America and Canada.

The Americans were great admirers of Jennie and Jane's quiet, stylish way of riding, and a few were surprised to learn that these elegant girls were also brave and capable cross-country. As soon as their hosts realised that they had been brought up in the great English hunting tradition, they invited them to follow an American pack of hounds, the North York hunt. The fact that they did not have foxes was no deterrent; they hunted anything that ran, which in this case, was coyotes. Jennie's greatest memory is of the incredible cold – the temperatures sank so low that they had to wear borrowed fur coats, which made them look like little bears on their borrowed ponies.

It would have been very easy for Jennie to have become big-headed, but working with the wild and woolly assortment of ponies at Catherston kept her feet on the ground. At any one time, there would be as many as a hundred animals on the place, including batches of ponies that would be bought in to be broken and sold. Learning to ride these was as valuable an experience as riding the made show ponies, and as a child Jennie probably learned more about educating youngsters than many riders learn in a lifetime.

Whenever she was riding, her little dog, Wuppies, would not be far away. Wuppies, immortalised in oils by Anne Bullen, was a Pekingese who had been given to Jennie by her grandmother – a caring but rather fierce lady whose image became linked in Jennie's mind with that of Boadicea, the warrior queen. Her imposing carriage and deportment were complemented by a deep voice; looking back, Jennie realises that she was a strong, determined, caring woman. She lived in Brixham, Devon, where she indulged her passion for sailing: she was intrepid to the point of pushing her skipper to sail out with her on seas that would prompt most people to keep their feet firmly on dry land. Jennie, who was petrified of her, remembers being taken to visit her and arriving to find her with a six-months-old puppy in her lap. She was told, 'Child, this is your dog' and Wuppies was handed over.

Wuppies was a particularly intelligent little dog, perhaps even psychic. He was very much 'Jennie's dog' and would go everywhere with her. She taught him lots of tricks and used to set up courses of small jumps that he would negotiate with an enthusiasm to match his owner's.

She remembers him with great affection and believes that he saved her life. The original Catherston was a big, rambling house and Jennie's room was some distance from the main downstairs living rooms. One night she was woken by Wuppies scratching on the bed to find that her room was full of smoke; somehow, the mattress had caught fire and was smouldering underneath her. Fortunately it had only just started and the fire was a slow burn rather than a rapid ignition, and though Jennie could not see through the smoke she was able to feel her way to the door, make her way into her parents' bedroom and alert them. Once they were sure she had suffered no harm, they managed to throw the bed out of the window and poured bucket after bucket of water over it. Next morning, Jennie had no bed left – but if Wuppies had not alerted her to the danger, she would probably have been overcome by the fumes before anyone else in the house realised what was happening.

There were numerous other occasions when Wuppies' 'sixth sense' let them know that something was wrong. One winter's day, when the children were having lessons with Mr Pulpher, Wuppies got hold of the bottom of the schoolmaster's trousers in his teeth and started tugging. The dog took no notice when he was scolded for such uncharacteristic bad behaviour and continued to tug, as if he was trying to get Mr Pulpher to follow him.

Not surprisingly, Mr Pulpher assumed that the little dog was being disobedient, but Jennie knew better. Deciding that Wuppies was telling them that something was wrong, she persuaded Mr Pulpher that they should let the Pekingese lead the way and followed him in the direction of the river. Wuppies was barking, which was a rarity, and when Jennie rode Mossy towards the sound she found that one of the ponies had found its way into the river and become trapped in tree roots. Wuppies was standing on the bank licking its ears and perhaps the pony found comfort in that, because it stayed calm whilst they dashed back to the house and found an axe to clear the roots. As soon as these were cut, the pony scrambled up the bank to freedom; though he could easily have broken a leg, he suffered no more than slight abrasions.

Jennie was alerted to a second potential disaster, again when she was riding, by Wuppies barking and insisting that she follow him. She discovered that one of their helpers had been riding out when her horse reared, coming over backwards between a petrol pump and a wall. Both were upside down, but the petrol pump prevented the horse from crushing his rider and probably saved her life. Thanks to Wuppies, who could not have seen the accident happen but who knew that something was wrong, both horse and rider were turned back the right way with no lasting ill effects.

It was at this stage of her life that Jennie first became aware of dressage as a discipline and a form of competition, though thanks to her mother's enlightened attitude the Bullen family knew from experience that a pony who was supple and obedient on the flat would be a pleasure to ride and more athletic in every way, including jumping. Riders like Lorna Johnstone and Mrs V D S Williams, who would later be so encouraging and helpful to Jennie, were the pathfinders for what many British riders looked on as something quite entertaining, but not as important or demanding as show jumping and cross-country.

For Jennie, the spark that lit the dressage fire was a performance at the 1953 Horse of the Year Show by Mme Lis Hartel of Denmark. In 1952, at the Helsinki Olympics, she was the first lady rider ever to be awarded an Olympic medal. Remarkably, an attack of polio eight years before had left her with residual paralysis in both legs, hips and hands and she had to be lifted on to her horse. To the spellbound Jennie, her display to music was so stunning that she was left determined that one day, she would be able to perform at the same level.

Writing in *Horse & Hound*, Mrs V D S Williams gave a knowledge-able and impassioned appreciation: 'Nothing but pure strength of will and unconquerable determination could have got Mme Hartel to the heights she has reached in dressage after her grave illness. One would think it would be difficult enough for her to ride an ordinary horse, but to ride with such skill a highly trained dressage horse and keep up such wonderful impulsion and long spells of passage is nothing short of miraculous.'

Two years later, Jennie had the chance to see Swiss rider Henri Chamartain – later a medallist in the Tokyo Olympics – again in a display. It seemed that for the great British riding and horse loving public, the only way they could feel comfortable with dressage was to categorise it as entertainment with an element of circus tricks about it, so that they could gasp in admiration at a horse performing piaffe or one-time tempi changes without appreciating the years of training and athletic ability needed to perform such movements. Jennie, who even at that age appreciated that dressage – albeit at a lower level – was the basis for every well-schooled horse or pony, had no such hang-ups.

She simply wanted to know how to do it, and though her natural shyness meant that she would normally find it hard to start a conversa-tion with a rider of this calibre, her thirst for knowledge gave her the courage. An even bigger hurdle was that Chamartain spoke no English, so Jennie was forced to call on every last reserve of her schoolroom French – which had centred on ordering meals in restaurants and asking directions to the railway station, not the niceties of dressage. Desperation bred inspiration; politely but seriously, she approached Chamartain and asked him if he would teach Mossy to perform piaffe, an advanced movement in which the horse takes elevated steps on the spot.

Amused by her determination, he agreed, and Jennie had to follow his instructions as best she could. They started by working Mossy in hand to establish the regularity of the steps and then Jennie was told to get on him again. Soon her pony was showing the beginnings of his first steps of piaffe, much to the delight of both Jennie and her teacher.

When you look at the popularity of dressage today, it is surprising to realise that even four years later, dressage was still very much a minority discipline. A *Horse & Hound* report from one of the big shows said that, 'Two delightful interludes were given by Mrs Lorna Johnstone riding Rosie Dream, her Olympic dressage horse, who gave many people the chance to see really top class dressage for the first time.'

In the same way that forty years later, endurance riders would have to endure gibes about 'long distance knitting' and assumptions that endurance was all well and good for those who couldn't do anything but hack, so dressage was thought of by some as an activity for those who were too old or too nervous to jump. The occasional enlightened voice, such as that of Lieutenant-Colonel J E (Jack) Hance, would protest the importance of dressage for every discipline: in the 13 October 1956 edition of *Horse & Hound*, he wrote that 'Only a short time ago we lauded the success of our teams at the Olympic Games at Stockholm, where we saw, or read of, the capabilities of half a dozen of our leading riders...all of whom admit that much of their success was due to dressage, either in its competitive form or as a means to an end in training their horses for the big contests.'

At the Stockholm Olympics, thirty nations were represented in the equestrian events by about two hundred competitors, who between them, had three hundred horses. Of those thirty, twenty-eight were entered in the Grand Prix jumping, twenty-two in the three-day horse trials and nineteen in the Grand Prix de Dressage. Britain won the three-day horse trials, to ecstatic reaction, with Major Laurence Rook on Wild Venture finishing second in the dressage section.

Britain's dressage hopes rested on Mrs Lorna Johnstone, Mrs V D S Williams and Mrs Esme Lascelles, though the latter was unable to ride because her horse, Achat, had a 'foreign body' in his leg which made him lame. After celebrating the horse trials gold medal winners' achievements over several pages, *Horse & Hound* managed a brief comment that 'Our two lady representatives put up a very creditable performance in the Grand Prix de Dressage,' adding that 'the judging system seems to have been well criticised.'

For the time being, competitive dressage had to remain an ambition for Jennie. There were no classes for junior riders, let alone junior riders on ponies, so she continued showing ponies for her mother and Miss Stubbings. By the time she was fifteen, she was rapidly outgrowing even the biggest of them, the 14.2hh ponies, and it was decided that it was time to move on to horses. In her usual 'We've made the decision, now let's do it' style, Miss Stubbings announced that she wanted to own a show hack.

Their travels took them to Newmarket in Suffolk, famous as the centre of the British Flat racing industry. There they visited a stud where Jennie fell instantly in love with a charismatic three-year-old dark brown mare who floated in trot around her field. Fortunately it was a unanimous decision, though there were times in the early days when it might have seemed to be more of an unfortunate choice.

Desert Storm, as she was called, was of Anglo–Arab breeding and so combined the beauty and grace of both the Thoroughbred and the Arab. Her sire was renowned for being difficult to handle, so it was thought prudent to send her to Major Pritchard, a well-known hunter producer, to be broken in. When she came back, it seemed as if she was following her father's example, but then it was discovered that one reason for her seeming waywardness was that she had wolf teeth – small, shallow-rooted vestigial pre-molars which the horse's bit may knock against, causing considerable discomfort.

Once these were removed Desert Storm became more relaxed, but as a four-year-old she was still difficult: it took another year for her to mature and show that she was after all a top class show hack. Jennie got to the stage where she could get the mare to go beautifully in and out of the ring, but Desert Storm had one major failing – she hated standing still. As the hallmark of a show hack is that it combines beauty and elegance with impeccable manners, this problem had to be sorted out.

Jennie's parents decided that the problem must rest with her, and that she must have an electric backside. This was not wholly fair, but making the transition from ponies to a horse of this calibre was bound to call for greater experience. This came via Jack Hance, the same person who had promoted the cause of dressage through the columns of *Horse & Hound* and who was a renowned trainer of show horses. He was a fierce and passionate man, and Jennie was terrified of him, but she also appreciated his brilliance.

Colonel Hance instilled in her the knack of sitting still and relaxed, but at the same time giving the horse confidence and quietly imposing discipline without setting up a confrontation. She lost count of the number of times he made her walk round the field, halt, ride on, halt again and talk to him, ride off again and so on until she and Desert Storm reached an understanding. The mare grew to trust Jennie and as long as she was in the saddle, standing still was no longer a problem. However, when the judge got on it was a case of hoping and praying – if he was not a particularly good rider, as was sometimes the case, Desert Storm would show her displeasure by leaping in the air.

Every horse you ride teaches you something, even if you are the one supposed to be doing the educating. Desert Storm taught Jennie how to insist on obedience, but in a way that the horse did not object to. As she points out to her pupils, riding any horse requires you to use your intelligence and common sense, but riding a mare can demand a little more skill and sensitivity than riding a gelding: as the old saying goes, you tell a gelding, ask a mare and discuss it with a stallion.

She and her daughters, Anne and Lizzie, have always been happy to compete mares and girl power is still very much in evidence at Catherston. They have produced a huge number of talented mares, including Wellingtonia, Anne's eventer, and Thean, who Lizzie competed in dressage to international level. Catherston Dauntless show jumped successfully with Johnny Harris then made an equally successful change to dressage with Lizzie. Catherston Jetstream was a successful show jumper, first with James Fisher and later with Lee Williams, and is now back at Catherston as a broodmare.

Much is said and written about the Continental practice of performance testing, but in Jennie's philosophy, horses should not only have
good conformation and temperaments, but whenever possible should
prove themselves in performance before they are used for breeding.
Over the years, this has produced breeding lines that have made their
mark on all disciplines, and horses that have competed against the best
in the world.

3

Against the Odds

The end of the 1950s was a time of change for the Bullen family. Running the estate had become an increasingly heavy responsibility, so Colonel and Mrs Bullen decided to find a new home that still allowed enough scope for breeding the ponies and for the girls to carry on riding and producing show animals. By this time the boys looked on riding as an important but perhaps not the major part of their lives, though Mike was making a name for himself as an event rider, so it also seemed the right time to reduce the number of horses and ponies – which then stood at about one hundred.

Many of the mares and youngstock were sold at Fayre Oaks sale, and Jennie was left in charge of Bubbly and the remaining horses and ponies. She stayed with her aunt, Lady Colefox, and travelled the six miles to their old home each day on a moped whilst her parents organised the transfer to Manor House at Didmarton, Gloucestershire. With the help of some of their former employees they transformed the Cotswold farmyard into a new stable block and on 1 April 1960, the name of Catherston Stud moved to Didmarton, complete with the two stallions – Bubbly and the chestnut Bwlch Zingaree, who had been bought as a good outcross to the palomino and dun mares by Bubbly – their brood mares and show ponies. Their new home had seventeen acres, which was perfectly adequate for their needs but must have seemed minute compared to the estate they had just left. Most of the horses and ponies settled quickly, with the exception of a

Dartmoor mare called Bo Peep. She seemed determined to find her way back to her old home and jumped the stone walls surrounding the fields in her attempt, sadly losing her foal as a result.

The move was in many ways a huge wrench, because the original Catherston had been in the family for so long, but Colonel and Mrs Bullen's sadness may have been tinged with relief that they no longer had the responsibility and expense of running such a huge concern. Forty years later, Jennie was to take a similar decision to step back from the Catherston of the millennium and find a way to run her life rather than let what had become an equestrian empire take over. It takes a particular form of clear sightedness to be able to see that, ironically, success has stopped you going forward, but in the case of both generations, it was the only way.

That same year, Anne Bullen was diagnosed as having cancer. Never one to complain or let illness or injury get in the way of family life, she could not ignore the warning signs and first consulted a doctor immediately after the Horse of the Year Show. Jennie and the others knew that she was ill, and over the next five years realised that she was getting worse, but although they were an incredibly close family the inevitable outcome was something they never talked about. It was enough to retain that closeness and to do all they could to help Mrs Bullen remain as active as possible.

This was made easier because, as everyone who owns horses or ponies knows, they impose responsibilities upon you. Even though there were fewer than when the family was at Catherston Manor, they still had to be cared for, schooled and competed. Without diminishing any of the seriousness of Mrs Bullen's illness, or its effect on the family, the commitment to their animals helped to keep a sense of continuity.

New owners joined Miss Stubbings to boost their string of winners. One of the most memorable was Elizabeth Profumo, an elegant, very attractive woman who was the sister of John Profumo. Her brother later became a household name when the affair that the newspapers soon labelled 'the Profumo scandal' hit the front pages, but Jennie has good cause to remember Miss Profumo as kind and generous. One of the best examples of this came a few years later, when Jennie and Anthony married and Miss Profumo paid for the installation of an indoor school. To make it easier for them to accept this magnificent gesture, she told them that she had always wanted one but had never lived anywhere suitable, so she would build it with them and leave it to them in her will.

All the Bullens were keen Pony Club members and regularly attended rallies at Highgrove, then owned by the Morgan-Jones family and now the Prince of Wales' home. Here they were taught by two legends in the eventing world, Colonel Frank Weldon and Colonel Babe Moseley, though it was only as they grew up that they realised how fortunate they were. Frank Weldon, in his heyday one of Britain's top riders, was director and course builder for Badminton Horse Trials for many years and was renowned for tearing a strip off any rider who he felt was not paying sufficient attention to his course briefings. 'Babe' Moseley was a big man whose round face and high speaking voice – quite out of keeping with his physique – gave him his nickname, but he too could strike fear into the heart of the most macho competitor. Jennie's most vivid memories are of his huge figure behind the wheel of his Bentley, which he drove with a cushion between his stomach and the steering wheel to prevent his coat buttons damaging the leather-covered wheel, and of his unvarying verdict on anyone who fell off: 'You did not keep hold of its head and ride'!

Paddy, the stud groom at Highgrove, instilled in them the basics of proper horse management, lessons that have remained with Jennie to this day. Students who find themselves criticised for not being able to muck out or groom a horse correctly have to admit that the criticism is justified when their boss shows how it should be done, and much of her technique is due to that wonderful old-fashioned Irish horseman. When Paddy had set fair a box, the centre would be deep and level and the banks around the sides high, and when he had finished grooming a horse, a hand wiped over its coat would find no trace of dust.

As a Pony Club member, Jennie enjoyed hunting and eventing and shared the others' enthusiasm for riding cross-country. Inevitably, there was the occasional spill, and just as inevitably there was only one thing to do when this happened – get up and get straight back on. In the autumn of 1959, an accident at a mock hunt had a far-reaching effect on Jennie's life, and what seemed at first like a disaster actually helped to shape her personality and give her a degree of confidence she might otherwise never have found.

It was one of those silly accidents that have no obvious cause. The going was fine, the conditions were good, the horse was usually reliable and the fence was straightforward. Jennie was at the back of the field making sure that all the younger riders got over the fence safely, but when her own turn came, everything went wrong. After a perfect approach, Jennie was thrown from her horse and hit the ground face downwards. Afterwards, she thought that the horse had somehow crossed his front legs on landing and tripped himself up.

Fortunately, there were no facial injuries, but the force of the blow transferred through her skull. Her next memories are of waking up in hospital, but later she found out that at first, it was thought she was unharmed. She got up and walked around, but later that day it was apparent that something was very wrong. She started saying things that made little or no sense and her parents were horrified to hear her urging Bonzo, the terrier, to jump out of the window, not realising what the consequences would be. Jennie was taken to hospital, where at first it was assumed that she was suffering from the effects of concussion. Farther investigations revealed that she had fractured her skull and a few days later she found that she had become ambidextrous and could write legibly with either hand; unfortunately, this potentially useful ability soon disappeared.

Jennie was told that the only answer was prolonged rest, which in itself was torment for someone so active. Worst of all, she was told that under no circumstances could she get on a horse for at least six months. She came out of hospital frustrated, fed up and longing to get on with her life. Academic work was not her forte – though the fact that she failed her only General Certificate of Education in English was due to a legacy of fear from the dreadful Irish governess rather than to any lack of intelligence – and the normally happy, common sense teenager found it hard to summon up enthusiasm for anything.

Mrs Bullen had read a newspaper article about the Duke of Edinburgh Award, which has now been undertaken by more than four million successful candidates but then had only just been opened up to girls. Under the patronage of the Duke, it was designed to nurture skills and a sense of achievement in young people by training them to undergo a series of challenges. These were divided into categories, including outdoor activities and work in the community, so that candidates had to demonstrate excellence in all areas and could not get by purely on, for instance, natural athletic ability.

With her parents' encouragement, Jennie decided to apply. The county youth officer for Gloucestershire, a sympathetic but definitely no nonsense woman called Miss Ruffles, came to Didmarton to interview her – a process which, at the time, seemed almost as demanding as the challenge it was all about. Later, Jennie realised that because the award had up until then been a solely male preserve, Miss Ruffles had to be sure that the first girls to enter were the strongest prospects she could find.

The next three years saw Jennie thrown into a whirlwind of activities and challenges. Some of them, such as party planning and elocution, now seem dated and irrelevant, but others were of timeless value. First aid and home nursing saw her spending a day a week working in a home for the physically and mentally handicapped and at Tetbury Hospital, work she found particularly rewarding. She says that if she had to live her life again and was forced to take a different course, she would perhaps have made nursing a career, though it would have been very much a second best to working with and training horses. Jane, on the other hand, knew even as a child that nursing was her vocation: later, when she was announced as a member of the British Olympic eventing team and had to combine preparations for Mexico with training at the Middlesex Hospital, the press dubbed her 'the galloping nurse'.

The physical activities were daunting, even for someone like Jennie, who was used to hard work and to being outdoors for long hours. As soon as she could start riding again, she incorporated her skills as a horsewoman into the Duke of Edinburgh Award. The family had bought a nice TB mare called Three Royals from Mrs Franks, who had sold Bubbly to them, originally with the intention of eventing her. However, Jennie had to find an area she had not specialised in before, and – not in the least put off by her earlier fall and its repercussions – decided to try race riding.

At that time, ladies could only ride in point-to-points, as the Jockey Club was not yet enlightened enough to allow them to compete against male jockeys in Flat races. Colonel Bullen had point-to-pointed in his youth; perhaps because he remembered the risks involved, he was not too happy about Jennie's new venture. However, his faith in his daughter's ability and the Bullens' belief that their children should be encouraged in anything they wished to do – as long as they were prepared to do it properly – overcame his reluctance. Once he accepted that Jennie was firm in her ambition and was prepared to work hard to achieve it, he encouraged her and made sure that every detail was as it should be.

They also persuaded Lawrie Morgan, a tough Australian event rider and Olympic gold medallist who also trained racehorses, to let her gallop the mare with his string and give her some tips on race riding technique. Jennie found the training as fascinating as the actual riding was exhilarating, and has been able ever since to draw on the skills she learned in getting horses fit. She set off for the starting post for the first time with the knowledge that whilst she might not be the most experienced jockey there, she had at least had a good grounding.

In her first race, she also had a slice of the luck that even the greatest jockeys need: coming into the last fence, she lay fifth and looked forwards to simply finishing the course according to plan, as she realised that Three Royals was tired. It seemed that the two horses immediately in front of her were even more tired – one fell at the last fence and the other refused, leaving Jennie to take third place. The next two seasons saw her ride a total of a dozen races, but although she was never unplaced and always came home in second or third position, she never managed to win. Point-to-pointing was the only equestrian sport in which she seemed destined to be always the bridesmaid and never the bride.

The Bullens later tried to breed from Three Royals, but with little success. She was sent away to stud but savaged by the stallion, so next time was introduced to Bwlch Zingaree. Her first foal was a nice bay colt who went to Jersey, and after that she produced a dun filly by

Bubbly which only grew to about 15hh and was broken and sold to the local vet for his children. After that, Three Royals decided she had had enough of motherhood and they never got her in foal again.

For reasons she cannot really explain, Jennie was determined that the Duke of Edinburgh Award would be the chance to confront some of her own personal demons, one of which was a fear of heights. When she passed the test in rock climbing, it was double the achievement. Jennie and the other trainees were sent to the Lake District on an 'outward bound' course, where a team of instructors was waiting to introduce them to canoeing and rock climbing. Jennie told no one of her fear, but the matter of fact encouragement of the instructors and her own determination allowed her to master it, even if she could not totally overcome it. Even today, she does not like looking down from steep heights.

Although she learned to cope with, though not enjoy, the climbing, she got quite a kick out of learning to abseil and by the end of the course was happily negotiating steep rock faces. If anyone had told her at the beginning of the course what she would achieve, she would never have believed it, but by learning to abseil in stages – first down a twelve feet drop, then gradually longer ones – she gained more and more confidence.

The rocky crags were a formidable challenge, but not the greatest: that came as part of her elocution work, when she had to memorise and quote prose and poetry. The fear this invoked was far greater than scaling heights could produce, because it brought back that terrible episode in her childhood when the abusive governess had inflicted such mental and physical pain. How could she explain that the reason the simple act of reciting a memorised poem reduced her to tears was that it re-opened such horrific emotional wounds – that every time she faltered, she was waiting for a crack of the whip?

The set piece, a poem entitled 'The Deserted Village', was one that she had been forced to learn before. Memorising it came easily and at home, Jennie was word perfect. But as soon as she had to stand in front of an examiner, she was panic stricken – she remembers two awful attempts when she simply could not utter the first line, and could only apologise through her tears. Finally, she became angry with herself, because she knew that if she failed this part of the test, she failed the whole of it, and her anger fuelled the breakthrough.

As she made her way to the examination room for the third time, the words of 'The Deserted Village' were ingrained on Jennie's mind. She knew every phrasing, every inflexion, every pause and could picture and hear herself reciting it as if she was watching a video of the actual event. As she greeted the examiner, she drove out every thought save that mental film and just a few minutes later, had passed one of the greatest ordeals she had ever faced.

Then, as now, the Duke of Edinburgh Award brings together people from all walks of life. One of the most enjoyable – and funniest – episodes was when Miss Ruffles announced that she had three girls who Jennie was going to take on an expedition. They were studying for their bronze award, whilst Jennie had been entered for the highest level, the gold, and taking on responsibility for them was part of her challenge. They had no idea of how to read a map, and it was Jennie's job to get the party safely cross-country, ending up at Prinknash Abbey in Gloucestershire.

As soon as they met, it was obvious that they were from very different backgrounds. Jennie was far shyer of them than they were of her, but knew that as the 'leader' of the party she had to establish a rapport. The obvious questions to ask were where they had come from and why they were doing the award, and all three came from the same place. Jennie had never heard of it and when she asked where it was, was cheerfully told that it was a prison!

The girls were all young offenders, but had proved that they deserved a chance to put right their mistakes. It was certainly the ultimate ice-breaker, and the trek was far easier than Jennie could have hoped for; she admits that for a fleeting moment, she did wonder what would happen if they decided to escape. She certainly learned as much about human nature as they learned about map reading, and the trip gave them all a real sense of achievement. The most difficult moment of the whole expedition came when they arrived at the abbey; catching sight of the monk coming to greet them, one of the astonished girls announced, 'Cor blimey, look at 'im – he ain't got no 'air on!' Elocution and party planning lectures had taught Jennie how to smooth over social difficulties, but unfortunately that one had not been included in the syllabus.

Three years later, Jennie received her gold award from Prince Philip, her first meeting with royalty. Although she was nervous, she was conscious of the honour and the Duke of Edinburgh spent a few minutes chatting with her about the training and how she had enjoyed it. Not only was she one of the first girls to undertake and win the award, she was the only one there who had done it as an individual rather than a member of a group or college. It would have been interesting to see her reaction if anyone watching that ceremony had been able to tell her that one day in 1968, during a celebratory party after the Mexico Olympics, she would be sitting on those royal shoulders in a swimming pool, kicking him in the ribs as he acted as her 'mount' in an impromptu game of water polo.

The girl who received her gold medal – something Jennie still treasures – was much more confident than the one who started the training. She had proved, above all to herself, that she could take on and overcome her worst fears, though she will always be inherently a shy person. It is almost funny to see those about to meet her for the first time, particularly those for whom her achievements have made her a heroine of the horse world, obviously in awe of her and not realising that Jennie is probably more nervous than they are!

Yet in competition she has never shown signs of nerves and has always been able to keep cool. This comes from her ability to focus on her horse and on the next few minutes in the arena, for which they may have been preparing for years. She can also concentrate on keeping her horse obedient and calm through her own body language, no matter how important the competition. This gift – or rather, a learned state of mind, because it does not necessarily come naturally – is something which marks out the great riders in all disciplines, from Mark Todd to John Whitaker and Lester Piggott.

Getting into the swing of working for the award helped Jennie survive the 'no riding' edict that the doctors had imposed after her fall, but she still felt like a fish out of water. As soon as she was allowed to get back in the saddle she made straight for her beloved Bubbly, because she knew that if things did not go exactly to plan she could trust him to look after her. This intelligent pony adjusted his way of going to whoever was riding him; he could be brave and bold for an experienced jockey, but quiet as the proverbial lamb if a child was put on his back. Soon Jennie felt that she was part of real life again, and was riding the show horses and schooling new prospects.

One of these was a scruffy, skinny little gelding who eventually grew another two inches and, in a real life rags to riches story that could have come straight out of a film script, became a top class event horse and won Badminton Horse Trials with Jane. A knock on the door one morning heralded the arrival of this unlikely looking future star, who had been boxed over to Catherston by the farmer who owned him. He had been told that Mrs Bullen had a knack with young horses – and although he did not say as much, it also became clear that he had heard that she might succeed where he had failed. With his lop ears and skinny frame, the youngster was little more than a pony, but he was actually pure Thoroughbred, by a stallion called Bewildered, and had not had a promising start in life.

His mother had foaled early out on the hills and he nearly froze to death, but gave the first hints of being a tough customer by surviving against the odds. As a two-year-old, under the name of Our Nobby, he raced on the Flat without much success and was then taken home. What happened to him over the next three years was not clear, but it soon became apparent that Our Nobby had a mind of his own.

The only reason Mrs Bullen bought him was that although he looked very unprepossessing when he arrived on her doorstep, her infallible eye for a horse told her that his basic conformation was good; once his hatrack frame was overlaid with muscle, his neck would not look so upside down and skinny and his big head and lop ears would appear in proportion. All of this proved to be true, though the ears – which prompted the family to call him Loppy at home – remained something of a trademark and the brain between them particularly sharp.

The first ten days were spent building him up with good food, as he could not start work until he had put on some weight. Loppy then caused the first of many problems by showing signs of a fungal skin rash. This proved to be ringworm, a highly contagious fungal skin infection that, despite its name, has nothing to do with parasitical worms. It spreads like wildfire and can be caught by humans as well as horses. By the time the diagnosis was confirmed, it was too late – all the show horses were showing the signs of round patches of scaly skin and the Horse of the Year Show was just round the corner.

These days, there are several drugs and topical washes to treat ringworm. Then, there was very little, though a drug called griseofulvin had just been developed and Catherston took part in one of the first trials. It undoubtedly helped, but they discovered that one of the most successful ways of killing off the fungi was to wash the patients in blue Daz, a popular washing powder whose manufacturers' advertising campaigns centred on its ability to get clothes 'whiter than white'. Somehow, killing off ringworm does not have quite the same aesthetic appeal.

Jennie, along with everyone else, became sick of the sight of it and 'washerwoman's hands' became a badge of honour at Catherston. The problem with ringworm is that it is spread by contact, which can be via tack, rugs, grooming brushes or countless other media. This meant that not just the horses, but all their equipment and surroundings had to be scrubbed and affected horses kept isolated from the others.

As soon as things were back to normal and Loppy was in better condition, Mrs Bullen decided to find out what she had bought. It soon became clear that the farmer had turned up on the doorstep not just on the offchance, but in desperation. The little horse was athletic enough, but he used his athleticism to his own ends – he was like an eel to sit on, and spectacularly nappy.

Someone had to sort him out and Mike, at six feet two, was nominated. The theory was that his height, weight and length of leg would enable him to show this self-opinionated overgrown pony the error of his ways, but Loppy disagreed. Watched in amusement by his mother and sisters, Mike was carted round the field at breakneck pace. It was surrounded by a four feet six inch post and rail fence, and on the first circuit everyone assumed that this would stop him. Instead, Loppy pricked his ears, jumped the fence in great style and proceeded to repeat the feat several times before agreeing to come to a halt.

At this stage, feelings were mixed about what they should do with him. Loppy obviously had an enormous jump, but equally obviously this was matched by an enormous ego. Mrs Bullen's understated verdict was that they might find him a little difficult to sell, so they had better keep him for a while and see what they could do. Like so many quirky horses, once he was in the right hands he turned out to be brilliant.

At first, Jennie and Jane shared the ride on him and cured his nappiness by taking him hunting, the traditional solution for horses who are reluctant to go forward or who have lost interest in life. Jennie hunted him for a season with the Beaufort, one of the smart packs, and recalls that he looked very small and scruffy at the side of the gleaming, plaited hunters. Nevertheless, he proved his ability by taking on everything this formidable hunting country had to offer and Jennie's only problem was trying to persuade him to go slower. Their performances across country were so impressive that Jennie was invited a wear the Beaufort coat, a great honour awarded only to the best performers in the field.

Eventually Loppy became more and more Jane's horse, because Jennie was busy with Miss Profumo's show horses and with Miss Stubbings' Desert Storm. It was Desert Storm, the aloof little mare who would only come to you if she wanted to, who began Jennie's 'proper' dressage career. She was a spectacular mover and spectators would gasp as she floated across the diagonal of the arena in an elegant but powerful extended trot. At the Horse of the Year Show, those in the audience were not the only ones to be impressed.

A team of riders from Germany had come over to perform a quadrille and though their Thoroughbred horses were impressive, Jennie was not so impressed by some of their riding, which left several horses with spur marks on their flanks. One of the lady riders saw Jennie and Desert Storm win their class and was so impressed by the mare's movement that she offered to buy her, with the aim of taking her back to Germany and competing her in dressage. For Jennie, this was a disaster: she had spent a long time building a relationship with Desert Storm and the bond between them was a solid one. She knew that the only way to succeed with her was through tact and quiet but firm insistence, and that any rider who took the attitude with her that 'You will do this' rather than 'Wouldn't it be a good idea to do this?' would end up with a battle that could only have one outcome, and it would be a very unhappy one.

Logically, she did not have a chance of matching the German rider's offer. Desert Storm was worth a lot of money, and the family finances, already stretched by the move to the new Catherston Stud and subsequent building work, could stretch no farther. Both Miss Stubbings and Miss Profumo sold their horses regularly because they wanted new faces for the show scene, and always found ready buyers. Nevertheless, Jennie went to Miss Stubbings and told her that if she was thinking of selling the mare, she wanted to buy her.

At first, Miss Stubbings was surprised; she knew Jennie had formed a strong relationship with Desert Storm, but was unaware of the depth of her feelings. With incredible generosity of spirit, not to mention financial generosity, she thought for a moment and then gave her answer: 'If that is how you feel about her, I will give her to you.' It was the start of a new career for both horse and rider.

Today, an introduction to competitive dressage is gentle and gradual for both horse and rider. At unaffiliated Preliminary level, the first rung on the ladder, tests are so simple that if horse and rider can trot and canter a twenty-metre circle and ride basic figures in all paces, they can ride a test even if they cannot expect to get good marks. Novice affiliated competitions ask little more in terms of the basics, though obviously the standard is expected to be higher and horse and rider to be able to give a more polished performance.

Even by 1959, dressage was the poor relation of Britain's equestrian sports. Competitions were few and far between compared to show jumping and eventing, and the idea that there should be a level at which the very novice horse or rider could be tempted into and enjoy the sport was not considered. The few novice classes on offer demanded work of a much higher standard than the modern version, but because Desert Storm was already so well schooled Jennie started out in advanced medium classes. Suddenly, showing seemed far less important: this was what she really wanted to do.

Dressage is said to be Britain's fastest growing equestrian sport, but at that time Jennie faced little competition. The only lady riders competing seriously were Lorna Johnstone and Brenda Williams, always referred to in print as Mrs V D S Williams; Jennie made up the third and most inexperienced part of that select band, later to be joined by Diana Mason. Because Jennie had trained Desert Storm to perform canter pirouettes and one-time tempi changes, changing the leading leg at canter with every stride so that the mare looked as if she was skipping gracefully across the arena in perfect balance, she was one of the few riders capable of representing her country at international level and found herself on the team for Hamburg, Cologne and Aachen.

At that time, Jennie's knowledge of training was based on what she had learned from her parents and a mixture of research and experimentation. She read books by masters such as General Decarpentry, Wilhelm Muhler and the then chief of the Spanish Riding School, Alois Podjhasky and coupled their advice with knowledge of her own horse. If one way did not work, she would try another until she got the results she wanted.

Travelling the horses would almost have counted as one of Jennie's Duke of Edinburgh Award assignments. The trips demanded fortitude, endurance and a sense of humour, as each took several days. The boat trains had no dividers – they had to take their own pole partitions and hang them from the roof – and the riders travelled in similarly basic style. Mrs Johnstone and Mrs Williams, who were generous with their time and encouragement for their young compatriot, had explained to Jennie that she needed to bring a hammock and showed her how to put it up; trying to sleep swinging from the roof was a skill you had to find out for yourself. The journey was farther complicated by the fact that animals and freight were only allowed to travel at night, and although the riders were allowed to leave the train during the day to buy provisions, the horses had to stay on board.

It was also thought inappropriate that Colonel Johnstone, who came to help his wife and support the team, should remain on the goods train at night with the women, so the poor man used to leave it in the early evening and thumb a lift in a passenger train. He would rejoin them at the first daytime stop, a system that worked well until one day the goods train did not stop at the station but in the middle of the countryside.

Their journeys were not over when they arrived at the main railway stations. Competitions were inevitably held some distance away, so they would unload the horses, tack them up and ride them through the city centres in the early mornings. Desert Storm might have been sensitive and at times temperamental, but her one unfailing virtue was that she was never frightened by traffic. Lorries could pass her with little room to spare and she would behave as if she was a police horse and in any case, traffic levels were less than a third of those we see today. The only thing that let her down was her old quirk of not wanting to stand still, so she had to be in front at traffic lights.

4

All-Round Horsewoman

Although dressage soon became the focus of Jennie's competitive ambitions, she remained an all-round horsewoman. It was not so much a conscious decision as a fact of life: the family had a stud to run and horses to produce and train and responsibilities had to be shared. None of this was a chore, because then, as now, Jennie's fascination with and enthusiasm for horses is not compartmentalised.

Over the past few years, she has been labelled first and foremost as an international dressage rider and trainer and breeder of competition horses. Whilst this is certainly the most public part of her life, she has always taken an open minded approach and is just as happy riding a mountain and moorland pony in her capacity as a showing judge as a Grand Prix star. Those riders who seem as if they want to file themselves under D for dressage might, perhaps, find that they and their horses could benefit if they took a similar outlook.

So whilst she was re-routing Desert Storm's career from the show ring to the dressage arena, Jennie was cheerfully juggling the many other facets of life at Catherston. One of these was handling and looking after stallions, which was actually ground-breaking stuff – though at the time, she did not think of herself as a pioneer. Dealing with stallions has traditionally been a male preserve, partly because there has always been a view that women did not have the strength to deal with powerful animals. Alongside that has been the assumption that it was not a suitable job for a woman, because of their supposedly more delicate sensibilities.

In the late fifties and early sixties the view that dealing with stallions was men's work was carved in stone. Part of this was down to practicality; for many years stallions were travelled to their mares rather than the mares being brought to the stallions. A stallion would stand in a district and be looked after by a stallion man, who would walk the horse miles from farm to farm. Although this would obviously not be practical or possible today, most studs still employ men to deal with the stallions and supervise covering.

However, enlightenment and common sense have always gone hand in hand at Catherston, and the Bullens' logic was simple: as the females in the household outnumbered the males, equality in the workplace was a fact of life. Jennie had been taught right from the start that establishing an understanding with any horse required kindness, fairness and mutual respect, but that one half of the partnership had to be in charge, and it could not be the horse. At fifteen, she was taught to look after the Thoroughbred stallion Golden Fern, who her parents had bought in 1949. When he arrived, Golden Fern was so wild he had to be chased off the lorry, but by the time Jennie came to deal with him he was much more civilised.

Although Colonel Bullen never felt the need to bully a horse, he knew that when it came to handling stallions, some men became over assertive and even aggressive simply because they were nervous of them. Whilst half a ton of all-male horse is not something you want to take liberties with, a horse who is treated like a wild animal will probably behave like one. Jennie learned through the example of her parents that if handler and horse have respect for each other the handler can keep the balance of power in his or her favour without the need for aggression.

Today, watching her everyday dealings with the stallions who have become such an important part of her life puts a new meaning on the words 'horse sense'. You will never hear Jennie talking in soppy, sentimental terms about her horses, but she has a bond with the special ones that most owners can only envy. One of the reasons for this is that she has the ability to think like a horse rather than trying to impose human values and attitudes on her horses – when a student trying to catch a mare with a foal at foot who did not want to be caught got between the two, he was left in no uncertain terms that Jennie was not impressed.

Later, he realised that the swift and immediate correction was for his own safety. A mare's instinct is to protect her foal, and if a human takes on the role of predator – which is precisely what the unthinking student was doing – those instincts will take over. A few sharp and unprintable words kicked his reflexes into gear and prompted him to get back in the safety zone, but another few seconds could have seen him being trampled. Because he realised that Jennie was looking out for him, the only lasting discomfort was to his pride.

The first half of the 1960s threw Jennie on to a rollercoaster of experience that underlined her strength of personality, or perhaps helped to forge it. For the rest of her generation, it was the decade that was to be labelled the swinging sixties and went from the sublime to the ridiculous: the Russians became the first to launch a man into space and bring him safely back again, Mary Quant invented the miniskirt, John and Robert Kennedy and Martin Luther King were assassinated. The world was in turmoil and so was Jennie's life, surging from moments of deepest sadness to newfound happiness.

It started in entertaining enough fashion. In 1960, Jennie gained her first experience of the excitement and unique camaraderie of the Olympic Games – not as a rider, but as a supporter to her brother, Mike. Mike had ridden his way into the top echelons of eventing with Colonel and Mrs Williams' Cottage Romance, and was picked to ride for the British team in Rome. It was the start of an incredible family sequence, because eventually three of the Bullens were to compete in Olympic Games.

Today, it is all too easy to look back at the competitions of forty or fifty years ago and dismiss them as presenting nothing like the challenge of those of today. In purely technical terms, that may be true; certainly the cross-country courses of the major three-day events

Mystic
gleam

A.B.

were nothing like as technically demanding as their modern counter-parts. But it is important to look at them in context – equestrian sport was much less commercial and the riders played on a much more level playing field.

Horses were not bought by companies for vast sums and produced for them by professional riders who did nothing else and could not survive without financial sponsorship. The Bullens were dedicated, knowledgeable and as professional as any others in the horse world, but it was professionalism in a different sense. Today, very few Olympic class riders have other occupations, because of the demands of the increasingly commercial world of equestrian sport. One notable exception was the late Reiner Klimke, a full-time lawyer who literally trained his horses in his spare time.

At that time, the Bullens were professionals in that horses were their life and as such, had to pay their way. But it was an all-round professionalism: they bred, broke and trained their own horses and those that were sent to them by outside owners were usually trained from scratch at Catherston. Today's top riders rarely have the time or the inclination to start from scratch with raw youngsters.

When you are trying to keep a sponsor happy by getting publicity for a company name, it is essential to score consistently and regularly at top level. This is where the publicity value lies: apart from racing, which is an industry rather than a sport, equestrian sports get abysmal coverage in the general media compared to football or cricket, even though top three-day events such as Badminton and Burghley attract crowds approaching a quarter of a million – perhaps twenty times the gate expected at top level cricket. Coverage of equestrian sports just one rung down the prestige ladder is even worse, and if you are looking for news of competitions which are the starting place for the international stars of tomorrow, you will find them only in the specialist equestrian press.

A horse has to be at least five years old to compete in pre-novice horse trials, the nursery school of eventing, and even if everything goes to plan, it will usually take at least another three to five years before he is competing at top level. Likewise, the established stars of the Olympic dressage arenas are usually in their early teens. For this reason, many riders prefer to buy horses that have already made successful starts to their competitive careers.

Anyone who has walked the cross-country course at Badminton or Burghley and stood in front of – or underneath – the imposing fences would be forgiven for thinking that the Olympic equivalent of 1960 looked much less of a challenge. However, whilst the courses were certainly not as technically demanding, the dimensions of the fences were the same as they are now; they were much flimsier and looked far less solid, which actually made them more dangerous. The Rome course was well within the capabilities of the halfbred Cottage Romance, who eventually came fourth, but the fences were badly made and several horses were injured.

Jennie, who was then seventeen, was invited by her cousin Vera to go and watch Mike ride. Hotels in Rome were at a premium and because they were two women travelling alone, they were given accommodation in a convent. Whilst they were out there, the British put on a Commonwealth dinner and she was asked by Mrs Moseley – wife of the formidable Babe – to take tickets at the door. Some of the show jumping riders were unable to attend, including Pat Smythe. Pat's husband, Sam Koechlin, should have been a member of the Swiss event team on Goya, a daughter of Pat's legendary grey mare Tosca, but three weeks before the Games Goya strained a tendon and put paid to their Olympic hopes.

Because there were spare places round the dinner table, Jennie and Vera were invited to stay, though Mrs Moseley gave Jennie strict instructions that she was to be Pat Smythe for the night. The dinner stretched out into a long and enjoyable occasion, and when it was finally time to say goodnight, Jennie and Vera realised that they were going to have to play Cinderella. The nuns, either because they were worried at the lateness of their return or because they knew more than they were letting on about Italian menfolk, greeted Jennie with the suspicious demand: 'Have you sinned?' Not sure what the correct or politic reply was, all she could think of was 'No, I've been out to dinner'!

Mrs Moseley bred, rather than bought, her show horses and all were out of the same mare, Swallow IX, by different stallions. Jennie's biggest victory for her was winning the Winston Churchill Cup at the Royal International Horse Show, which was then and is now one of the most prestigious awards in the showing calendar. Her partner was Highland Fling, a big, beautiful horse who was a picture in the show ring but who Jennie remembers best for being 'as thick as two short planks'. He was the equine equivalent of the stereotypical dumb blonde, all looks but with very little between the ears. However, his impressive movement and wonderful looks could not fail to impress the judges, though Jennie had to be careful to keep him calm and confident in what he was doing. If he was asked to do more than his limited brainpower could cope with, he would panic – and a horse of that size running away without realising either why he was doing it or what he was running from was no fun if you happened to be sitting on him.

In 1962 the Moseleys decided to see how their show horses fared on the other side of the Atlantic. In an account written two months afterwards, Mrs Moseley describes their 'whirlwind five weeks in America and Canada…all of us agree that every moment was unforgettable and supremely worthwhile.' She acknowledges that the speed of their departure was only made possible by Colonel and Mrs Bullen's help and advice, and by their allowing Jennie and Charlie to join them. Michael Bullen, a partner in Peden International Horse Transport, made all the travelling arangements for the three horses, Diddikai, Flight of Fancy and Highland Fling.

Diddikai was Mrs Moseley's hunter and though a big horse at 16.3hh, looked comparatively small at the side of his two half brothers. The six-year-old Highland Fling stood 17.2hh – a giant of a horse for someone of Jennie's size – whilst the year older Flight of Fancy, who was to be Charlie's ride, was even bigger at 18hh. First stop was Washington DC, where Jennie, Charlie and Mrs Moseley were signed up as guests of Mr 'Stretch' Harding at the Congressional Country Club. The horses were four miles away at the newly built Potomac Horse Center, which boasted an indoor dressage arena surrounded by loose boxes and galleries.

The horses settled in remarkably quickly considering that there had been a ten-hour delay on the airfield, and whilst they had a couple of days to acclimatise, their riders watched the dressage competitors of the Washington Horse Show riding at the Potomac arena. One of the highlights was seeing Henri Chamartain – the Swiss Olympic medallist who had helped Jennie introduce Mossy to piaffe – and American rider Jessica Newbury practising their pas de deux, which they performed each day at the show.

Soon it was decided that Mrs Moseley's horses would benefit from a quiet, relaxing walk out in the surrounding countryside. The horses themselves were working to a different agenda and expended their pent-up energy in bucking, snorting and prancing their way along the route, much to the entertainment and fascination of their hosts. The Americans were amazed not just at the horses' freshness, but at their size: Mrs Moseley records that the average American horse stood at little over 15hh and most were Thoroughbreds.

Showing hunters in the States was and still is very different from showing hunters in the UK. All were required to jump, and though they had managed one schooling session over show jumps before leaving England with Molly Sievewright, founder of Talland School of Equitation in Gloucestershire, they knew it would be a case of playing it by ear. Jennie was the most experienced rider over jumps, but had Fling's lack of experience – and, to be honest, brains – to cope with.

Mrs Moseley records that most owners of show hunters in the USA employed professional trainers, and the riders, too, were mostly professionals. The horses were carefully schooled in their speciality and most began their jumping training as three-year-olds. The classes were divided into three divisions, each with different requirements; conformation classes were judged on jumping performance and the horse's conformation, working hunter competititions on jumping performance and style only and green hunter classes, for horses in their first and second years of showing, were formatted to take into account their lack of experience. Diddikai was entered for the conformation division, Flight for the working hunter and Fling for the green hunter section.

The sartorial demands on the riders were equally complex. Classes were farther categorised as Corinthian or non-Corinthian, and in the Corinthian classes, men were expected to ride as 'an MFH, whipper-in or member of a recognised Hunt'. Ladies astride donned silk hats, 'shadbelly' or 'weazelbelly' coats with cutaway fronts and Hunt collars, buff breeches and black boots. Jennie and Mrs Moseley were given permission to wear their blue and buff hunting coats, hunting breeches and silk hats. Mrs Moseley wrote that at forty-six, she flatly refused to sport a 'weazel' or any other kind of belly!

Not surprisingly, they could not compete with the specialists on home ground, but put up good performances and left with a coveted ribbon for fourth place in the hunt team class. Morale had risen rapidly by the last day of the show, when Colonel Moseley joined them and delivered an affectionate but brutally honest summing up to his wife: 'Our horses are much too big, and you are too old, my dear'!

The next stage of their adventure was the New York Horse Show at Madison Square Gardens. Here even more of the crème de la crème of American showing talent was on display, but though there were no more ribbons to add to the one from Washington, they did themselves and their horses justice. They also learned how to prepare an American tack box, a cross between a tack room and a display room where visitors could look round and converse. It was impossible to compete with the scallop-edged, appliqued canvas walls and chandeliers of home exhibitors, but they lined the walls with blue and buff bunting, miniature Union Jacks and photographs from hunts and shows.

An amazing number of visitors passed through the tack box, looking at the equipment and the horses and sometimes offering to buy the latter. They wanted to know how the horses were bred, what it was like hunting in England and how they stopped their top hats become furred up. Mrs Moseley wrote in obvious delight that they accepted most of the answers, 'but could not believe that the perspiring elderly person "spitting and polishing" our boots was really the owner and breeder of the three horses, who firmly and frequently stated that she had no intention of selling any of them.'

The final leg of their showing tour took them to Canada, to the Royal Winter Fair in Toronto. Here the Moseley horses really came into form and on the first day alone won first, second, fourth and fifth ribbons, which were added to throughout the show. In the final class, Jennie excelled herself by jumping the biggest – over four feet six inches – and most difficult course they had faced so far, riding the 18hh Flight. They took home with them a fantastic collection of memories and experiences, from the warmth and friendliness of the American horse world to the food – hot dogs, hamburgers, clam chowder, waffles with maple syrup and ice cream sodas. Even Babe, whose appetite was as large as his girth, admitted that he found the size of the helpings too generous.

Soon after Jennie's return, it became clear that Mrs Bullen's illness was taking its toll. She fought against it with determination, characteristically refusing to let it interfere with family life or her work. Sadly, she could not hold it back forever and from about the middle of 1963 became increasingly weak as the cancer, which had spread throughout her body, devastated her spine. She continued painting for as long as she could manage, and her last painting was of some of the horses and ponies as she visualised them outside her window.

Eventually it became necessary for a nurse to be in the house twenty-four hours a day and though Mrs Bullen did her best to hide the degree of pain she suffered, Jennie and the others realised that it was getting

Above: Sarah Bullen riding Prosperity of Catherston. Bred by Thalia Gordon-Watson, she was by Bubbly out of Fortune II and was a major influence on the pony scene of the 1960s (*Monty*)

Right: Jennie riding Rosalind at the Royal Counties Agricultural Show. Rosalind was a difficult pony but went on to produce some lovely foals when she was sold to the Dilkes family (*Graphic Photos*)

Above: Jennie and her favourite pony Mossy about to compete at a hunter trials (*Regent Photographs*)

Left: A generation later: Jennie's daughter Anne with Mossy

Right: Jane Bullen
jumping Our Nobby
over fences at home

Below: Our Nobby being
trotted up for the vets'
inspection by groom
Jennie at the 1968
Mexico Olympics

Above: Desert Storm about to enter the ring at White City

Below: Desert Storm and her first foal, Desert Star, at Catherston Stud in the New Forest

Right: Mrs Moseley's Highland Fling who floated through the mud to win the Hunter Championship and Winston Churchill Cup at White City

Below: (*left to right*) Charlie Bullen on Flight of Fancy, Jennie on Highland Fling and Mrs Moseley on Diddicoy in New York (*Budd*)

Above: Wedding day, 27 February 1965; Anthony and Jennie with Anthony's mother and Jennie's father (*Van Hallan*)

Below: Bubbly's son, Double Bubble, with Anne and Lizzie

Above: Xenocles, Jennie's first thoroughbred stallion. A kind and gentle horse, he won jumping, dressage and eventing competitions

Below: Miss Profumo holding her hack Midnight Sun. With her is Anne aged two-and-a-half

Jennie and Kadett at Fontainbleu – her first international win (*Photo Delcourt*)

The day of the massacre at the Munich Olympics; Jennie and Kadett (*Mitschke*)

worse. Over the last few months of that year Mrs Bullen grew increasingly weaker and towards the end became delirious, not recognising members of her family. When she died, on 22 December, it was an irreparable blow to her husband and children but also a release from the pain which had taken over her life.

The Bullens were one of those rare, remarkable families where their overall closeness was echoed by the individual bond between husband and wife. Jack Bullen was sixteen years older than Anne, but although they were very different in character they were the two halves of a successful and loving partnership. She was a rare mixture of the intuitive, the creative and the practical – wife, mother, artist and businesswoman, whose energy and determination shaped the lives of her children in ways that she would have been proud and satisfied to see.

Her loss was devastating. Colonel Bullen did his best to keep going as she would have wished, but found it impossible. Looking back, Jennie believes that he never came to terms with his grief and though he did his best to help them carry on with the stud and the horses, his heart was no longer in it. Anthony and Charlie were by now both working in businesses unconnected with the horse world, and as the eldest sister, Jennie tried to be strong to help Jane, Sarah and herself pick up the rapidly unravelling threads of their lives and hang on to the family unity that had always kept them so secure.

At that time, Charlie was going out with a girl who used to work for the family. The marriage lasted ten years and produced two much-loved children, Elizabeth and Kate, but eventually Charlie and his first wife started to drift apart. For a while, Charlie lost his closeness with Jennie and the rest of the family, but this was only temporary. Jennie, who could not bear the thought of her brother being alone at Christmas, issued an invitation to lunch and made it quite clear that a refusal would not be accepted. Charlie took little persuading and any rift was soon healed. Some time later, Charlie met Sarah Hickson, later to become his wife – a marriage that has brought happiness to both of them.

Today, Charlie and Sarah run a stately home in Winchester that was once the home of Sarah's parents and is the focus of a favourite family story. Sarah's father was an army colonel who was stationed in Burma, and during a period of leave he and his wife decided to come home to look for a country cottage. They spent days looking at various properties, none of which matched up to the picture in their minds, and eventually he had to return to his post.

His wife carried on looking and, according to family legend, the bemused colonel received a telegram saying 'Found our cottage. A little big, but can make a living from it.' When it became clear that the 'cottage' was actually a mansion house, his commanding officer sent him home on compassionate leave – but it became a happy home for Sarah, and later for her and Charlie.

Charlie, whose business interests include building cross-country courses, has always had a fascination for machinery – and according to Jennie, is the human equivalent of the cat with nine lives. She says he used up one of them as a little boy when he had the accident that nearly tore off his arm, and another soon after leaving school, when he joined a company called Scottish Land Developments. This was started and run by a man named Niall Hodge, who left home with the proverbial £40 in his pockets and became a multi-millionaire through hard work and a gradual venture into earth-moving equipment.

To a machinery enthusiast like Charlie, driving huge diggers and getting paid for it was a job made in heaven. He nearly ended up there sooner than he thought, when he drove too fast up a huge slag pile and found himself sitting in a machine that was slipping down the side with an avalanche pouring down on top of him. Fortunately, other digger drivers were able to get him out before he suffocated.

His fascination with how machinery worked also led him to start his own garage business, repairing cars. Like most one-man businesses, this took hard work and long hours before it started returning a modest profit – but even this was threatened by a series of break-ins. Charlie knew that a group of local yobs was responsible and decided to show them that interfering with his livelihood was not a good idea.

Although he was not an aggressive young man, he was not frightened to stand up for himself and when a confrontation with the burglars got really nasty, refused to back down. One of them threatened him with a knife, but Charlie swung out with his 'bionic arm' – which after all his operations and implants virtually had a steel core – and laid him out. The rest did not wait to find out whether this was good luck or if they had taken on more than they had bargained for, and Charlie's business remained undisturbed from then on.

Michael Bullen's business career has been spectacularly successful, but he has also had to cope with disaster. In partnership with James Peden, he started an animal transport business that developed into one of the best known names in international horse transport, flying racehorses round the world and looking after horses going to the Olympics. Its reputation was worldwide and no one – least of all the Bullens – could believe what was happening when Michael was arrested on a complicated charge relating to fraud over an aircraft. Michael's family and friends knew that there could be no substance in the charges and one of his friends, Mark Barlow, put up bail. The worst thing for Michael was that his good name had been cast into doubt. When the case came to court, he was completely exonerated, and though no one who knew him had dreamed of any other verdict, it was an incredibly stressful time.

Even worse was the time a straightforward charter ended in disaster. Michael was waiting for an aircraft with three of his men and a large number of horses to land and as he watched it come in to land he realised, to his horror, that something was wrong. A mechanical fault in a wing flap caused the plane to veer out of control and it crashed into a terminal that was under construction. Three men, all valued members of his team, were killed along with eighteen horses.

In the August of 1964, Jennie was twenty-one. At that time, this birthday marked your 'coming of age,' the official transition from adolescence to adulthood. The loss of her mother and the ensuing responsibility she felt both for her younger sisters and the continued success of Catherston meant that her carefree childhood was already part of her past; it was not that her father did not do his best, but he was heartbroken when Anne Bullen died and never managed to find the same interest in life again. However, appreciating that it was important to celebrate this special birthday, and knowing that it was something his wife would have wanted, he was happy to agree when

Mrs Moseley said she wanted to give a party for Jennie.

It turned out to be one of the most important days of Jennie's life, because it brought about the first proper meeting with the man she was to marry. Anthony Loriston-Clarke was tall, handsome and attracted the eye of more than one female guest, but it was Jennie he wanted to meet. He insists that it was actually the second time their paths had crossed – the first was at another party, way back in their childhood. His very first sight of his future wife was as she slid down a polished corridor on her bottom, egged on as usual by Charlie!

It must have been hard to reconcile the image of that little tomboy, decked out in her best party dress and with her hair curling down her back, with the attractive, still slightly shy young woman celebrating her twenty-first birthday. Slim and elegant, wearing a light green dress with an Elizabethan neckline – a birthday gift from Miss Profumo that she still has – Jennie also wanted to find out more about her guest, and their meeting sparked off an attraction that neither quite realised at the time was mutual.

Jennie admits that she thought Anthony, who did his National Service in the Navy where his father was a captain, and had been out to the Far East, was 'a bit special'. Shortly after the party, when she received a letter from him, she realised that perhaps he felt the same. Until then, any boyfriends had been regarded merely as friends, but her feelings for the then twenty-eight-year-old Anthony and his for her soon became much deeper.

For the first two months of their relationship, meetings had to be fitted round Anthony's work commitments; as a metallurgist, he was at that time involved with developments in hovercraft. Jennie continued to help keep Catherston running smoothly, albeit on a smaller scale. For some of the time, letters were their only way of keeping in touch and, in the time-honoured way of younger sisters, Jane and Sarah took great interest in the romance's progression. They also served as an excuse to tease Greta Phillips, who – no doubt mindful of how the girls must be feeling the loss of their mother – came one day to see how they were getting on.

Jennie and her sisters remember Greta with great affection, but also because she never stopped talking. Jane and Sarah decided to sidetrack her, and when a letter arrived for Jennie, knew that this was their chance. They knew very well that it was from Anthony, but handed it across and casually told Jennie that she had another letter from Prince Ali of Mahishabad, confiding in Greta that he looked incredibly handsome in his long white costume.

Poor Greta was dumbfounded and almost had a nervous breakdown at the thought of Jennie marrying an Indian prince. Overcome with worry, she told Anthony that he had an exotic rival – but Anthony, who had been let in on the secret right from the start, was able to reassure her. Greta was so relieved that it was a very long time before she remembered to tell them off for their teasing.

There was no doubt in either Anthony or Jennie's minds that this was more than a casual romance, and when Colonel Bullen took Jennie and a Dutch au pair, Dieneke Vos, to Venice for a much-needed holiday, Anthony managed to get enough time off to join them for the last four days. Everyone realised that the relationship had moved on to a serious level and there was little surprise when they announced that they were getting married. It might have seemed like a whirlwind romance – the wedding was just six months after they had met – but Jennie and Anthony had no doubts that they wanted to spend the rest of their lives together.

They were married in Tetbury Church, but on the day Jennie had no time to be nervous. A marquee had been put up in the garden at home with heaters to dispel the February chill and one of the heaters was sited too close to the wall; as Jennie was in her room starting to get ready, a waiter came rushing up to the house shouting that the tent was on fire. Pausing only to pull on her dressing gown, she flew down the stairs to find her father and the waiter doing good impressions of the agitated white rabbit in Alice in Wonderland and had to urge them to fetch buckets of water to quench the flames.

After that disastrous start, the marriage ceremony came as something of a relief. As she entered the church with her bridesmaids – Jane; Sarah; Anthony Bullen's daughter, Catherine; Mrs Moseley's daughter, Jennifer and Dieneke – Jennie's only worry was that she would tread on or spill something on her wedding dress, which was and still is a family heirloom passed down through her father's side of the family. Made from antique cream satin with Brussels lace overlay and a train, it has one section from a dress made for an early eighteenth century bride, with additions from the mid-1800s and 1902. Later, it was to be worn by Jennie and Anthony's younger daughter, Lizzie, but on 27 February 1965 Jennie Bullen walked down the aisle to add to its history by becoming Jennie Loriston-Clarke.

5

Highs and Lows

Jennie and Anthony spent their honeymoon in Switzerland, returning home via Holland. Miss Stubbings suggested that rather than leave Desert Storm idle, this might be an opportunity to let the mare do some work with a Dutch trainer in Holland and for Jennie and Anthony to pick her up on the way home. Right from the start, it was clear that no one expected marriage to interfere with Jennie's riding commitments!

Happy as Jennie was to enjoy time with Anthony, when the time came to return home she was also pleased at the thought of being reunited with Desert Storm. They organised their return to fit in what was meant to be a quick stop to collect her, only to walk into a nightmare. The trainer, who had seemed so plausible and so charming to Miss Stubbings, turned out to be a conman.

Miss Stubbings was an astute woman, but she and everyone else had been completely taken in. The trainer claimed that she had sent Desert Storm to him on a permanent basis to continue her training, and for a few short, nerve-racking days Jennie was worried that she might not get her back. Finally, Michael Bullen stepped in and took legal action to make the mare a 'ward of court' so that the trainer could not spirit her away.

Jennie was able to reclaim Desert Storm and take her home, only to discover that her problems were not yet over. Those few weeks away had wreaked a terrible effect on the mare's sensitive temperament and as Jennie put her back into work, it became clear that she was so traumatised and over-trained that she had lost all trust in her rider. She was tense, unsettled and sour and though Jennie spent many patient hours trying to restore the delicate balance, Desert Storm never fully came back to what she had been.

Jennie and Anthony's first home, Black Knoll, was owned by Anthony's mother, Cicely, who generously offered not only to share it with them but to turn her garage into a flat for Jane and Sarah. It must have been a dramatic change in Mrs Loriston-Clarke's lifestyle, but Jennie says that although she must have wondered what had hit her, she made them all welcome.

By then, Jennie owned two horses, Desert Storm and a lovely TB stallion, Xenocles. Xenocles came from Nora Wilmot, then one of the older generation of trainers who was reputed to be an excellent judge of a horse. When Jennie explained that she was looking for a younger animal to bring on and lessen the load for Desert Storm – who by then had probably reached the limits of her training – Mrs Wilmot suggested she look at a beautifully bred, good looking entire who on paper should have won the Derby. Unfortunately for his racing connections, Xenocles moved too high off the ground when he galloped, which was not conducive to maximum speed.

However, his other talents blossomed in Jennie's care. He became not only a Prix St Georges dressage horse but an advanced eventer, and Jennie remembers him with great affection because he would always try his best for her. His generous attitude to work was coupled with a kind temperament and his greatest friend was the stable cat, who would sit on his back and dab at his mane with his paws. One morning, the cat grew a little too cheeky even for the tolerant Xenocles and sat in his manger eating the stallion's feed. Jennie saw Xenocles pick up the cat very gently in his teeth, carry him over to the door and deposit him on the ground outside with equal care.

On another occasion, when her eldest daughter, Anne, was a toddler, Jennie walked on to the yard to find that someone had tied Xenocles up in his box but left the door open. A confident Anne, who came barely up to the stallion's knees, was picking his feet out with a hoofpick whilst Xenocles behaved like an old patent safety pony.

Thoroughbreds have a reputation for being 'hot', but Xenocles was one of those rare horses who, in Jennie's words, you could gallop one minute and dressage the next. He was a fabulous mover who showed a natural talent for piaffe and passage, but was very sensitive about being asked to perform flying changes. Jennie insists that if she knew then what she knew now, she would have been able to overcome this sensitivity; even so, it was a rare achievement for a young rider to take a colt out of training and educate him to such a high level in both disciplines. His offspring inherited his temperament and versatility: Xenarchus, who was out of an Anglo-Arab mare, was an advanced dressage horse who competed in the European Championships and Autumn Folly, out of Judy Crago's great show jumping mare, Spring Fever, jumped at international level.

Whilst Jennie and Anthony were based at Black Knoll, Jane looked after Bubbly and Bwlch Zingaree at Catherston, helped by Oonagh Corscadin. Oonagh had been groom to Colonel and Mrs V D S Williams, who owned Cottage Romance – Michael Bullen's mount at the Rome Olympics. This was only a temporary arrangement, as Jane was determined to make a career in nursing and was accepted as a student at the Middlesex Hospital in London.

Looking to the future, Jennie needed more land and when a farm five miles away with twenty-eight acres came up for sale, she and Anthony managed to buy it. Pear Tree Farm came with one big drawback – the land seemed to consist mainly of ragwort, which is lethal to horses and causes slow, insidious liver damage. Jennie's abiding memory of that time is spending hour after back-breaking hour pulling up the deep-rooted plants with their deceptively attractive yellow flowers and burning them.

There was a stable and three stalls – old-fashioned accommodation in which the occupants are tied up and unable to move around – at Black Knoll, but they were not suitable for Desert Storm. After a quick transformation worthy of the BBC's *Changing Rooms* the garage became her new luxury home. Later on, Anthony, with the help of friends, spent six weeks' leave building eight luxury stables from forest cedar and when Jane started her nursing training, stalls were transformed into stables for the two pony stallions.

One of the friends who helped build the new stables was trying to decide her future whilst helping Jennie and Anthony start theirs together. Deeply religious, she eventually entered a convent but as the time came to take her final vows, acknowledged that she was not sure whether she was ready to commit herself totally to the Church. Sensibly, she went on retreat to a remote island monastery to try and discover where her convictions lay, and met a monk who was in a similar mental predicament. They found their solution in an unexpected way, by leaving their respective orders and getting married.

In July 1965, Jennie competed Desert Storm in Aachen. She thought she must have picked up a stomach bug, because she felt so nauseous, but fellow competitor Jook Hall had another explanation. 'You're pregnant,' she told Jennie, who realised that she must be right. Both she and Anthony, who had gone to Aachen with her, were delighted and she was confident that she would be able to care for the baby and still pursue her riding career. It seemed that life was offering a welcome chance of stability, and when their daughter was born on 19 January 1966, Jennie and Anthony decided to call her Anne.

Jennie had carried on riding as normal for the first four months of her pregnancy, but then hormones kicked in and began to affect her nerves. She no longer felt confident jumping and recalls that she also hated being a passenger in a car; she became what she describes as the worst ever back seat driver, but fortunately this state of mind disappeared when Anne arrived.

Realising that her riding had been affected, Jennie decided during the last months of her pregnancy that she would be better to concentrate on working horses from the ground. Anthony's mother helped her keep Desert Storm fit by hacking her round the forest, and enjoyed having lessons on her with Jennie. It was whilst they were in the school one day that Anne decided it was time to make her presence felt, and half an hour later Jennie was in Fenwick Hospital, Lyndhurst.

The arrival of his first grandchild was a delight for Colonel Bullen, but still he never recovered from the loss of his wife. Later that year, he was in the middle of selling one house and buying another in Dorset when he had to go into hospital for an operation. He came through it seemingly without any problems and when Jennie went to see him in the afternoon she came away relieved that he was more cheerful than she had expected and looking forwards to leaving hospital. It was an enormous shock for her and the rest of the family when he died the next morning, as suddenly and quickly as if he had fallen asleep.

Jennie's only comfort was that her father's great friend, Dr Campbell, was with him. Later, the doctor told her that he walked in to see Mr Bullen, who greeted him with a simple 'Hello' – then quietly died. Jennie was convinced, afterwards, that her father had simply had enough of life; he was heartbroken when his wife died and it was as though the knowledge that his daughters were safe and together gave him the freedom to go.

In a year and a half, Jennie had experienced more highs and lows than most people could bear. Her life at that point reads almost like a Shakespearean tragedy – losing her mother, then marrying and having her first child before the death of her father. Yet she turned out to be far stronger than any dramatist would expect his heroine to be, despite the depth of her feelings and the strength of the bonds that had kept the Bullen family so close.

With Anthony and Anne, she had a new life to follow. But she also had her brothers and sisters to grieve with – and in the case of Jane and Sarah, to feel responsible for. Anthony and Michael dealt with the business side, but caring for Jane, Sarah and the horses fell naturally to Jennie. There are only five years between Jennie and Jane, but at that stage in their lives the timespan encompassed a wide gap of experience and knowledge. If Jennie acquired a maturity beyond her years, it was because she had to in order to keep going.

It was important for the sake of continuity that Jennie and Jane continued to keep Catherston's name well-known in the equestrian world. In 1968, Jennie and Desert Storm were short listed for Britain's team for the Mexico Olympics, and because there was a shortage of top level competitions it was decided to hold one at Catherston. It was a far cry from the top level competitions that were held at the Catherston of the 1990s, with its indoor and outdoor schools and all mod cons and most of today's horses and riders would probably have had joint nervous breakdowns. The going was perfect, on old forest turf, but the venue came with unwanted spectators – forest ponies who happily wandered across the arena, regardless of any rider who happened to be performing a test at the time!

In the end, it was Lorna Johnstone on El Guapo, Johanna Hall on Conversano Caprice and Dominie Lawrence with San Fernando who eventually wore the Union Jack on their coats. At least on this occasion, we had a team: at the previous Games in Tokyo in 1964, Mrs Hall was our sole representative. Jennie was disappointed not to win a place, but knew in her heart of hearts that though Desert Storm had the ability to be an Olympic dressage horse, her temperament was not reliable enough. If she had never gone out of Jennie's hands, the story might have been different, even though Jennie says she does not think that in those days she knew enough about training to progress such a sensitive horse to the highest levels. That, however, is academic: those few weeks with the Dutch conman had done irrevocable damage.

However, she did not have time to brood over what might have been, because Jane and her little, lop-eared hooligan on four legs made '68 a year to remember – for all the good things, this time. Keeping Our Nobby fit was a joint effort, because by now Jane was nursing at the Middlesex Hospital, running up and down the stairs to build her own fitness and coming home between shifts whenever possible to ride him. Jennie worked him in her absence, recalling all the skills she had built up when getting Three Royals ready to point-to-point. It was a mixture of faith, hope and downright determination when Jane came off night duty at the Middlesex and rode Our Nobby to win the country's premier horse trials in her following four days off – from bedpans to Badminton. Their win, and the way it was achieved, made their selection for the Mexico Olympic Games almost automatic and with Jennie as groom, they won a team gold medal for Britain.

That, together with a silver medal from Britain's show jumping team, sent Britain's reputation as an equestrian nation soaring. Even those who knew nothing about horses regarded the two girls – Jane and Marion Mould, who rode her way into the legends by winning the individual silver medal on the 14.2hh Stroller – as heroines. In Mexico, the celebrations included a swimming pool party where the riders' competitive spirits were chanelled into a game of water polo. Jennie, co-opted on to one of the teams, was hoisted up on to a pair of strong male shoulders and was soon caught up in the enthusiasm, kicking her human 'horse' in the ribs to urge him on. She looked down and remembers thinking that the head of thinning hair looked slightly familiar, though she could not quite place it. A few minutes later, she realised that she had been drumming her heels on a pair of royal ribs – her partner was the Duke of Edinburgh.

It was inevitable that Jennie, whilst overwhelmed at Jane's success, should dream of Olympic honours herself. Finding the money to buy a horse with this potential remained a dream for the next two years, until one day just before the Christmas of 1969 Gill Steele came to visit the stud and suggested that she should buy a horse for Jennie to ride so that, as the owner, she could share the excitement of top class competitions.

Jennie knew that she no longer wanted to concentrate on showing, and Mrs Steele was just as happy to become involved in dressage. The hunt began for a potential partner, with Jennie asking all her contacts in the slowly growing world of dressage if they knew of anything with potential for sale. She wanted a horse that she could compete on at relatively high level as soon as she had formed a partnership with it, but did not want someone else's reject or a horse who had been made sour – criteria that are as difficult to satisfy today as they were then.

Eventually word came via the equestrian grapevine of a horse in Holland who might be what Jennie was looking for. Fellow dressage rider Sarah Whitmore was trained by Franz Rochowansky, a former chief rider at the Spanish Riding School who first came to Britain in the 1950s to hold clinics. Then, dressage was just a foreign word and only an enlightened few realised how lucky they were to have access to someone with such a wealth of knowledge and ability.

Rocky, as he is affectionately known, was born in Vienna and has a rich ancestry that is a mixture of Czechoslovakian blood. Even in his eighties, he was still riding two horses a day and working several others in hand, and dedicated his life to dressage. At the same time, he expected dedication from his pupils and in his earlier years was famous for his fiery temper, albeit coupled with enormous charm.

But whilst he made few allowances for people, Rocky's talent for bringing out the best in any horse was legendary – so when Jennie heard that a horse he had trained up to advanced medium level was for sale, she was immediately interested. The horse was a ten-year-old Trakehner cross Thoroughbred gelding, just under 16.2hh and was offered for sale because his male owner was too large for his lightweight frame.

Trying to find the right horse can be rather like waiting for a bus: it takes seemingly ages to track down anything sounding remotely suitable, and then either three come along at the same time or you have to jump through hoops to get on the one you want in time. So it was here, because Rocky had only one week to sell the horse; if he was not successful, it was to be sent on to Germany. The situation was complicated even farther by a postal strike and everything had to be done by telegram; Sarah Whitmore sent Jennie a telegram to say that she had found a horse that could suit her and that it was there for ten days, so she needed to see it quickly.

Unfortunately Jennie was suffering blackouts and was unable to go. She had been riding Wayfarer, a 17.1hh gelding which Mike had evented, on walk exercise to start his return to fitness after a tendon injury when other riders cantered up behind them. Although she

managed to keep control, Wayfarer's jerking at the reins set up a problem in her neck – a problem which, though Jennie did not realise it at the time, was to have much greater repercussions.

It was decided that Sarah Bullen and Mrs Steele would go and look at the horse, who was called Kadett. They thought that although he was obviously not the easiest of rides, Jennie could build a rapport with him, and her next potential dressage star arrived without her ever having sat on him. Kadett was spooky and sensitive and early attempts to teach him piaffe made him panic – not because he had been bullied or coerced, but because he was that sort of horse. If Kadett had been a person, he would have been a prime contender for an ulcer.

When she got him home, Kadett tested not only Jennie's patience, but her inventiveness. Looking back, she says that coping with the challenges he presented helped her enormously with other horses, but at the time he could be frustrating to the point where it was a competition to see which of them could outsmart the other. Kadett was always spooky, but as she got to know him, Jennie learned that this side of his nature was, in part, an evasion.

If she trotted him round on a loose rein he would stay relaxed and everything would be hunky dory, but once she picked up the reins and told him it was time to do some work, he would decide that things going on outside the arena that had been perfectly acceptable before were suddenly frightening. Yet the thin line between insisting that he pay attention and work correctly and setting off one of his 'panic attacks' was no more than a hairsbreadth. Riding Kadett was a balancing act, at times exasperating but never dull.

Then, as now, Jennie often succeeded where others would have given up by finding unconventional ways round training problems. One of Kadett's party pieces was to leap in the air for no reason, usually because he did not want to do something. Rather than tell him off and set him on a rapidly tightening spiral of tension and worry, Jennie's solution was to school him out on the forest, where there were lots of gorse bushes. She would deliberately work him round the bushes so that if he performed one of his vertical take-offs he pricked himself on the gorse, but when he behaved himself patted him and gave him lots of praise.

Kadett might have had an 'artistic temperament,' but he was not stupid. By ensuring that bad behaviour became associated with discomfort and that life was much nicer and more comfortable if he behaved, Jennie got her message across in the most effective way. Most important of all, the discomfort came not from her but from his own behaviour.

An equally unconventional approach enabled her to solve the problem of Kadett's piaffe. This is one of the most demanding movements, requiring power, collection and perfect balance as the horse 'trots on the spot,' lowering the croup, lightening his forehand and flexing knee, hock and fetlock joints. It is a two-time movement, but at first Kadett performed his own version in four-time – which may have been a contributing factor to his panics about it, as he lost track of what his legs should be doing!

Jennie wanted to put him in a situation where he would work out for himself the most comfortable way of performing a correct piaffe. The best way to do this, she decided, was to ride him in the river. She started by taking him as deep as possible without him losing his confidence and asked him to piaffe; the drag of the water meant that he had to move correctly to keep his balance, and self preservation took over. Once he had the idea, she asked him to work in gradually shallower levels, until he was as happy in piaffe on dry land as he was in the river.

In the last ten years the horse world has turned enthusiastically to trainers such as Monty Roberts, who are often given the romantic label of 'horse whisperers.' No one would argue that Roberts and the few others of his calibre have a lot to teach us about horse psychology, body language and so on. But whilst we tend to think of this as a new phenomenon, Anne and Jack Bullen were using instinctive horsemanship skills like these as a matter of course, and passing them on to their children.

The difference between them and Monty Roberts and co. is that Colonel and Mrs Bullen, and later Jennie, thought of what they were doing as a mixture of horse sense and common sense. In one way they were absolutely right, but their skills were rare ones – they might not have analysed what they were doing or given them names such as 'join-up' to try and make them accessible, but there are remarkable similarities between what the Bullens were achieving half a century ago and the so-called 'new approaches' of today.

Juggling horses, the stud work and family commitments was a permanent balancing act. When Jennie went to competitions, accompanied by Anthony whenever he could manage it, Anne would sit in her pram by the lorry. She was a happy, easy-going baby who loved horses and gravitated towards them as soon as she was old enough to toddle round the yard. Both she and later Lizzie had a network of adoring uncles and aunts and grew up surrounded by achievers and adventurers.

Anthony, the oldest of the Bullen children, was never particularly interested in horses. His passion was planes and flying, but sadly he was unable to achieve his ambition of joining the Royal Air Force because his eyesight did not meet their stringent requirements. However, he was a competent pilot with his own licence.

One morning when Anne was about four years old, Jennie had left her watching television whilst she caught up with some chores in the kitchen. Anne wandered into the kitchen and told her that Uncle Anthony was on television because he had been in an accident. Jennie rushed through and caught the end of a news item showing a small plane which had crash landed.

As there was no farther mention of the pilot's name, or whether or not he was safe, she rang the police. They could not help, so Jennie contacted the BBC. After an agonising wait, they confirmed that Anthony had indeed been the pilot and had been taken to hospital with a fractured skull. Later, he explained that it was only when he was taking off that he saw that wire used to winch up gliders was lying on the airstrip. This caught round his plane's tail wheels and caused the accident.

Just as Anne Bullen had always been in demand as a teacher, so Jennie found that her skill in the show ring and the dressage arena attracted would-be pupils. Soon after she started establishing her partnership with Kadett, Jennie became pregnant again, this time with Lizzie. Both she and Anthony were delighted but towards the end of her pregnancy, she inevitably had to stop riding. Rather than put Kadett's working programme on hold, she worked him from the ground, keeping him supple and giving him enough to think about.

Soon after Lizzie was born, in July 1970, Jennie was back in the saddle and back on course for her Olympic ambitions.

Whilst Jennie was establishing her career, Anthony was a respected metallurgist. He had worked on Concorde before meeting her and then went on to work with hovercraft. After that, he lectured on metallurgy at the College of Higher Education in Southampton and was called in as a consultant on the *Torrey Canyon* disaster in 1967, when a massive oil tanker struck rocks off the Isles of Scilly and caused the worst oil slick ever known. The damage potential to the environment and particularly to seabirds was enormous and Anthony helped formulate ways of turning the oil spill into a 'mousse' that could be skimmed off the top of the water.

Catherston still had to pay its way, though, and its earning potential was increased by taking in horses and ponies at livery to be broken and schooled. Equine students were joined by human ones and Catherston's name was to become a byword in training for anyone who wanted to work with horses. Jennie feels that sometimes there is little difference between the two and four-legged students, as it is a case of giving them something to think about, showing them that it more pleasant to do things the right way and – occasionally – turning unruly young hooligans into civilised personalities who are pleasant to be with!

The students were usually not much younger than Jennie, but the training environment then was much less structured and relied on learning through experience and example rather than through formal examinations. Jennie says that the best lessons came from the horses themselves, and that training was more of an apprenticeship: students came, learned the ropes, and when they were good enough to make a practical contribution, got paid! Rather than a 'them and us' situation, it was more of a team set-up, with the boss shovelling as much manure as the students.

Her strongest memories of those days are that it was fun, because no one was frightened of hard work – if they were, they did not last long. As far as she was concerned, as long as everyone pulled his or her weight there was no need for formality, though she has fond memories of her mother-in-law worrying that it might not be a good idea to let the students call her by her Christian name. Mrs Loriston-Clarke's tentative suggestion that perhaps 'Mrs Jennie' was a more suitable appellation was politely ignored by her daughter-in-law!

Occasionally, routine gave way to the decidedly out of the ordinary. In 1970, when Jennie was just a fortnight away from having Lizzie, she got a phone call from her brother, Mike – who was then running what quickly became one of the best known international horse transport companies, Peden, transporting racehorses and competition animals throughout the world. Mike cheerfully announced that Catherston had to get ready to welcome twenty-two bullfighting Andalucian stallions and their grooms, members of a display team from the sherry-producing capital of the world, Jerez.

Sponsored by Humberts, the local sherry importers from Southampton, they were to give a display at the Royal International Horse Show. The logistics of the operation would have been enormous at the best of times, but when their visitors arrived, it took on a decidedly comic dimension. First of all, the grooms themselves could not muster a word of English between them, though their constant smiles helped to make up for it, and no one at Catherston knew any Spanish apart from *Ole*! When the visitors saw that Jennie was in such an advanced stage of pregnancy, they were touchingly anxious on her behalf, bemused that a woman in her condition could think of being so closely involved with horses. Jennie, as always, could not bear to sit still and watch others do the work, so was trying to do as much as possible.

The stallions, striking looking greys of about 15hh to 15.2, were amazingly well-behaved. In Spain and Portugal, countries which retain their macho culture, stallions are regarded as the only suitable mounts for men: mares are for breeding and geldings are mounts for women and children. Whilst Andalucians have a natural fire and presence in their looks and movement, they generally have exceptionally kind temperaments and at the local horse fairs, stallions will be tied up in lines next to each other, without barriers between them and without problems.

For them to arrive in England and be installed in loose boxes with automatic watering systems was a culture shock, akin to taking a child who has been raised on a remote Scottish island and has no concept of a city and suddenly putting him down in the middle of London. At home, these stallions were kept in stalls and led to water twice a day; the grooms arrived with two huge glass bottles with long necks, which were tipped up so that the horses could drink from them. Now they had the freedom to move around their stables and water available all the time; they seemed to get used to and appreciate the former, but water on tap took more understanding. The novelty of automatic waterers, which generate fresh water whenever the horse puts its nose in the drinking bowl, obviously appealed and the horses enjoyed them so much it was as if each had a permanent fountain in the corner of its stable.

Soon after they arrived, one of the grooms appeared at the house and by repeating 'Medico, medico,' with accompanying extravagant gestures, indicated that he needed medical attention. Anthony took him to see the local GP, who also could not speak Spanish, and they entered into a game of medical charades. Through some inspired guesswork, Anthony realised that the poor man was suffering from some sort of urinary problem! A prescription swiftly solved his problem and for the rest of their stay, the groom looked on Anthony as his personal saviour.

Before they set off for London, the grooms showed their thanks by putting on a special show which translated as being 'good luck for the baby.' Out came the carriages and the ornate harness of the driving horses and the equally ornate saddles and bridles of the ridden ones. The horses wore fearsome looking bits with long cheeks, but were ridden on the weight of the reins alone with the aids being given via changes in the rider's weight.

After a breathtaking display by a driving team of five horses, three in front and two behind, one of the grooms gave a ridden show. It was a memorable experience for Jennie as she watched him perform all the movements that are used in fairs and parades, as each rider tries to show the spectators that he is the best rider with the best horse. For the finale, she was given a bullfighting display with one groom and a unicycle mounted with horns on the handlebars taking the part of the bull whilst horse and rider performed half passes, pirouettes and turns on the haunches.

It was spectacular showmanship, but it also showed the common link between horse lovers of all followings and all nationalities. It also demonstrated the common truths that so often become lost when competition becomes the be all and end all of a rider's life – that dressage means training the horse to achieve agility, balance, suppleness and harmony with the rider, and that the advanced movements are as natural to the horse as trotting across his field. Jennie might never have had to avoid a charging bull, but probably could if she had to.

6

Passing on the Knowledge

Just as Anne Bullen's skills in producing horses and ponies had led to her becoming in great demand as a teacher, so more and more often Jennie found herself asked to give lessons to riders who wanted to emulate her success, both in the show ring and the dressage arena. Until her late twenties, she had never thought of taking any British Horse Society examinations – mainly because exams of any kind were such an ordeal. She would rather have faced the legendary wild animals from her childhood woods than sit in an examination room with the clock ticking away.

She also admits that she had been fairly lukewarm about the traditional exam system, mostly because she had met so many people who had all the qualifications on paper, but were not particularly useful when it came to practical horsemanship. However, when she sat down and thought about her future she knew that teaching would eventually play an increasing part.

The lessons of her childhood also kicked in. Time after time, her parents had showed her that if you wanted to criticise something, you had to be sure that you were speaking or acting from an informed position. The more she thought about it, the more Jennie realised that there was only one thing to do: work her way through the system so that she was in a position to judge it from the inside rather than the outside.

Eventually, she was to gain the highest award the BHS can give: the fellowship, for which candidates can only be examined by those who hold the title themselves and which is recognised throughout the horse world as its highest accolade. The first step, though, was to gain the dreaded assistant instructor (AI) qualification, and to start with Jennie was worried that her lack of O-levels would be an insurmountable problem. However, she discovered that because she was over twenty and had proved herself in so many areas, this stipulation did not apply.

She was pretty sure that she would not have any problems with the riding part of the exam – after all, if you are riding at Grand Prix level and have been shortlisted for an Olympic team, you are hardly likely to encounter difficulties riding school horses accustomed to everything the weekend novice can put them through. The mechanics of teaching, though, were a different ball game and Jennie realised that this was foreign country. Although she knew nothing about it, she knew a man who did: Paul Fielder, now an accomplished rider and trainer himself, but then working as a groom and rider at Catherston. In a sporting and sometimes amusing spot of role reversal, Jennie persuaded him to give her lessons; Paul took his duties conscientiously and later never took advantage of the fact that he could truthfully say he had taught Jennie Loriston-Clarke!

Then, as now, the BHS exam system looks at the practicalities of running a riding school as a business as well as testing teaching and horse management skills. Although she was familiar with running a stud, Jennie did not know if or how this would relate to running a teaching establishment, so organised some private lessons with a friend called Melissa Morgan, who was a qualified BHS instructor. At that time there were just two levels of basic qualification, the BHSAI and the BHSI; later, the intermediate instructor qualification was added.

When the dreaded examination day came, Jennie could at least be confident that she had acquired a grasp of the riding school industry. That did not stop her feeling nervous and when she arrived at the centre and had made herself known to the owner, the next important step was to find the loo. Its unsavoury nature was the first hint that whilst this might be an examination and teaching centre, it was not exactly up to the standards the BHS was supposed to promote.

After an initial talk with the examiners, Jennie was presented with a horse to ride. It was second nature for her to check its tack before she got on, and it took only a few seconds for her to realise that one of the stirrup leather buckles was broken. Deciding that she was damned if she did and damned if she didn't, she was not prepared to ride under those circumstances and pointed out how dangerous it was.

It was difficult to tell who was the most embarrassed, Jennie for having to point it out or the examiners for discovering the low standards at what was supposed to be a model of teaching excellence. A new pair of stirrup leathers was fetched and fitted, a relieved Jennie got on board and the riding part of the exam passed without incident. Looking back, she says that the examiners were probably so mortified she would have had to get on facing the horse's tail for them to criticise her riding.

The next part of the exam was the section Jennie was most nervous about, the teaching test. Three guinea pig riders rode into the school and after the examiners had briefed her on the areas her lesson was to cover, she asked them to warm up their horses.

To her horror, as soon as they went into trot she could see that one of the horses was lame. By now she was not sure whether to laugh or cry, but one thing she was sure of was that she could not ignore it. Deciding that a little diplomacy was called for – and that the best way to get out of this was to put at least some of the onus on the examiners – she went up to one of the assessors and said that one of the horses did not appear to be sound, and what would he like her to do? She was told to restrict that horse to walk work, and the rest of the lesson passed off smoothly.

Jennie jokes that after such a catalogue of disasters, the examiners would not have dared to fail her. One thing that is certain is that she was the first and probably the last BHSAI to have been shortlisted for the Olympics! Although that first qualification made little if any difference to her ability to teach, it was the first step towards establishing Catherston as one of the most influential teaching centres in Britain.

The next career progression on the teaching front came in 1976, when Jennie took her full instructor's qualification. The intermediate

Chiquita + family, Chicakan, Boozy + Chi-ack.

exam had yet to be devised, though the BHS did arrange training sessions and conferences for talented riders and trainers working through the system. Jennie remembers one of these, at Stoneleigh, particularly well, mostly because it developed into a noisy and slightly heated discussion session.

The subject under scrutiny was gadgets or training aids, mechanical contrivances such as draw reins supposed to make it easier for the rider to work the horse in a correct outline. In skilled hands they may sometimes have a place, but unfortunately they are more likely to be used by the inexperienced desperate for a 'quick fix'.

There are two sides to every argument, and on this occasion Jennie found herself on the opposite side of the debate from Richard Davison. Richard was later to follow Jennie's lead in becoming a fellow of the BHS at an early age – in fact, he became the second youngest fellow after her – and was a member of the British Olympic team at the Sydney Olympics in 2000. His view was that gadgets were an essential part of every tackroom, whilst Jennie maintained that there should rarely be a place for them. Eventually, they had to agree to differ.

Jennie remembers the instructors' exam chiefly because, in her own words, she made 'a right Horlicks' of the show jumping phase. She had just returned from the Montreal Olympics and could not remember the last time she had jumped a course. Her riding had been so focused on dressage that there had been no time to get back in the swing, so all she could do was hope that her earlier years point-to-pointing and eventing would hold her in good stead.

She was presented with a horse and asked to ride him in and assess what she thought his capabilities would be. He seemed a useful sort and was a responsive ride on the flat, so after jumping him over a cross pole, a small upright and a larger spread – the only practice jumps she was allowed – Jennie told the examiners she thought he would be a pretty good performer at Foxhunter level. Foxhunter classes were devised to introduce young and fairly novice horses with natural talent to jumping more substantial fences. They demanded more than Newcomers classes, which were then the first rung on the affiliated show jumping ladder, but were not as challenging as the 'proper' grade classes.

Once she had given her assessment, the examiners asked if she would be happy to jump round a course set at Foxhunter level. Jennie agreed and at the first fence her horse seemed to prove her right, flying over it in great style. Unfortunately, when they reached the second fence he slammed on the brakes with equal enthusiasm and Jennie's only consolation was that she managed to stay on.

She had a split second to decide whether to give the horse a whack and try again, or admit that perhaps she had overestimated his ability. Relying on the instinctive certainty that punishing the horse would be the wrong decision and would only make things worse, she calmly told the examiners that she had been too generous in her original reading and now felt that the horse was only ready to compete at Newcomers level. The course was lowered and riding as positively as she could to give the horse confidence and let him know that there was no way he was going to be allowed to refuse again, they produced a copybook round. She was satisfied and so were the examiners, because they passed her with only a throwaway comment that her show jumping skills seemed a little rusty.

In 1978, Jennie was invited to take her fellowship. Someone once described this as the equestrian equivalent of a knight being asked to prove that he was worthy to sit at King Arthur's round table, and as long as you discount any ideas of Holy Grails and damsels in distress, there may be a grain of truth in this comparison. Just to be invited to take it was, and is, an honour in itself, as candidates can be assessed only by those who already hold the accolade.

Although it was the most demanding of all the exams Jennie had taken, it was also the most enjoyable – if an exam can ever be enjoyable. Although she was being watched and assessed all the time, it was on much more of a one to one basis, by people who were ready to listen and seemed genuinely interested in what she thought. The riding section involved each of the half dozen candidates getting to grips with horses that had been brought in for the day from a local dealer's yard. These were ridden in the open, first to assess their standard of schooling – or lack of it – and then over jumps. It soon became clear that they were a very mixed bunch.

Some were reasonably schooled, but in the case of one or two it was pretty obvious that they were in a dealing yard because it was the only place where their owners could get rid of them. Those who were matched up with the more civilised ones to start with could only count their blessings for a short time, as the examiners made them swap horses to prove that they could adapt their riding technique as necessary.

For Jennie, accustomed to riding so many different sorts of horses and with the gift of being able to persuade a naughty or stroppy horse that it actually wanted to do what she asked it, this was less of an ordeal than for some of the other candidates. The part of the exam which worried her more was the twenty-minute lecture – not just because she hated speaking in public, but because she had been warned that the biggest hurdle she had to overcome was keeping Colonel Crawford, the chief examiner awake. He was renowned for falling asleep in the middle of candidates' presentations, which could hardly have been encouraging.

Jennie had decided to lecture on the subject of training stallions as riding horses, because it was an unusual subject but one she had great experience in. She prepared her lecture notes carefully and rehearsed their delivery with Anthony before the exam so she could speak fluently and confidently. However, what kept Colonel Crawford awake was her assertion that a stallion could have a roving eye, but when he was under saddle everything else had to be kept in its proper place!

At the end of the day, she went home happy that she had done her best. Now she had to wait for the results: as she discovered later when she was on the other side of the fence, as an assessor rather than a candidate, a lot of discussion goes on afterwards. Of all the BHS exams, the fellowship is unique in that candidates are judged by their peers – and as Jennie points out, it is sometimes difficult to assess people whose specialities are different from your own. When Jennie took it, candidates had to have a broad base of riding ability and experience so that, for example, even those whose main interest was show jumping would have to demonstrate that they could ride at Prix St Georges level. Now, it is angled towards a more specialist approach.

When the letter came to tell Jennie that she had been awarded the fellowship, she felt that all the work had been worth it. It was an achievement by any standard, but an even greater one if you looked back to the little girl who battled against dyslexia, the teenager who conquered her greatest fears to speak in public and go rock climbing and the young woman who was convinced she would be unable to take her BHSAI because she did not have any O-levels.

The more teaching she did, the more she enjoyed it. She is renowned for being able to tailor her approach to the individual rider, just as she is able to get the best out of every horse by taking into account its temperament and individual strengths and weaknesses. Not surprisingly, most of her pupils are dressage specialists, but she gets as much satisfaction from 'talent spotting' a youngster with a hairy pony as from her clinics throughout the world.

The only thing she asks is that whatever level her pupil is working at, he or she is prepared to work and to accept that mistakes are inevitably the rider's fault, not the horse's. Whether she is teaching an amateur rider or a national team member, she puts in the same effort and gets the same satisfaction from their progress; one woman visits her five or six times a year for lessons on a horse she has brought on from scratch. At the end of each lesson, Jennie sketches out a work programme for her for the next two months, and because the rider follows this conscientiously is able to move on with each lesson. It might take this pupil years to reach a stage that others who can manage more regular training sessions can get to in months, but that does not detract from either her or Jennie's enjoyment or sense of achievement.

In dressage, as with all equestrian sports, there is a percentage of spoiled brats with mega money ponies who are only interested in turning up to competitions and winning. Jennie is more interested in the talented youngsters whose parents cannot afford expensive ponies and have to work with what they can afford. On one clinic, she spent a lot of time with a teenager determined to make the most of her nice but very ordinary New Forest pony; as Jennie pointed out, it may never have the paces of a 'mini warmblood,' but by helping the girl to bring out every bit of its potential she was teaching her a way of working and riding that might one day win her rides on better ponies and horses.

It is not that she is in any way snobbish about the sort of animals her pupils should ride, and can appreciate a good Mountain and Moorland pony as much as a good warmblood. Ann Birche, the rider of a wonderful Haflinger stallion called Oxnead Aristocrat, who competes at advanced level, says that when she took him to one of her clinics, Jennie was full of enthusiasm for him. Harry is a wonderful example of his breed and of the correctness of Ann's training, but a lot of less knowledgeable people would have turned up their noses at a little stallion of barely 14.2hh.

Jennie is adamant that neither horses nor riders should spend all their lives in indoor schools and says that her horses have always stayed sane because they got out and saw the world. They did much of their schooling on the forest and were expected to work with all the distractions around them, from forest ponies to pigs. As Jennie says, how can you expect a horse to cope with competition surroundings and atmosphere if it only sees the same arena every day and is carefully shielded from anything that might make it spook or shy?

She feels strongly that too many people now try to specialise before they are ready. Even if they are not brave enough to jump, or do not enjoy it, they should be able to ride their horses in all circumstances. Sadly, she finds that even children are starting to say 'I do dressage' rather than combining dressage with all-round riding ability and enjoyment. If

Jennie had never gone hunting, played at circus routines with her ponies and learned the stickability and reactions needed to ride cross-country, she would not have become the dressage rider and trainer she is today.

Recently, she was at a competition where a rider was asked to warm up on grass before going into the arena. He looked horrified and exclaimed 'But my horse never goes on grass!' as if the steward had asked him to perform the impossible. To Jennie, this sort of attitude is negative thinking. Whilst it is ideal and in some circumstances essential to have access to an arena with good going, she encourages her pupils to stay in the real world and to incorporate schooling into hacking or when riding in the field.

When Jennie first started competing, all the Grand Prix competitions were on grass because very few people had artificial arenas. And when the Loriston-Clarkes first arrived at the third Catherston Stud in Hampshire, they trained all the horses on grass because there was nothing else; the indoor and outdoor schools had not yet been built. They turned it to their advantage: they schooled in the top field because by the time they had trotted up the hill the horses were settled and warmed up and could get on and work. Transitions between paces had to be ridden according to the conditions and riders had to think.

Because she has seen so many pushy parents who try and live out their own ambitions through their children, Jenny has always been careful not to put too much pressure on her own daughters. When Anne was little, there were no formal lessons as such. Instead, she and Jennie would do what they called 'a bit of practice' for ten minutes – quite enough for a four-year-old's concentration span – interspersed with hacking. Going out for a ride with mum meant that Anne could practice some of the things they had done in relaxed surroundings and enjoy herself at the same time.

Teaching her daughters helped Jennie to develop what is now her instinctive knack of matching the approach to the rider, because although both Anne and Lizzie showed great ability from the start, they were very different in their attitudes. Anne was fearless and loved galloping and jumping, and decided early on that she wanted to specialise in eventing. Lizzie, who is now an international dressage competitor in her own right, was much more timid and at first, far more interested in grooming ponies than riding them.

She now has the same cool head and unflappable nerve as her mother and is quite unperturbed by the antics of a young stallion starting to feel a bit 'macho'. But in the beginning, she was far more interested in ballet than in horses and used to go to ballet lessons with a friend's daughter. As a little girl, she was so thin and gangly that the family affectionately nicknamed her 'Stick Legs'; now she is enviably slim and elegant, though the elegant exterior hides a steely determination that Anne Bullen would have recognised and appreciated.

Conscious of how important it was that her children enjoyed their riding, Jennie was thankful that she had the perfect first mount ready and waiting in her beloved Mossy. Although he was 13.2hh and Anne's legs came barely halfway down his sides, he was a perfect gentleman and, says Jennie, taught her far more than she could have learned through formal instruction. Soon she was riding him off the lead rein; she also rode Bubbly in equal safety, remarkable proof of the little palomino stallion's wonderful temperament.

Although both ponies were totally trustworthy, they were really too big at this stage, and Jennie looked for something smaller. The answer came – via Sarah Whitmore, who had helped find Kadett – in the shape of a wonderful Welsh Section A pony. A striking chestnut with four white socks, he rejoiced in the name of Twyford Salvo, but quickly became known as Dinky Toy at home. He cost £100 and at first, Jennie began to wonder if he was more trouble than he was worth: he was ticklish, nervous, a monster to break and totally unsuitable for a child. But with time and patience, he matured into a wonderful lead rein and first ridden pony.

Anne Bullen taught her daughters to ride side-saddle as well as astride, not because it looked elegant but because it gave them extra security on larger ponies. Jennie rode 14.2hh show ponies, which are almost little horses, at the age of eight and enjoyed riding side-saddle throughout her riding career until back pain made it impossible.

Today the art of side-saddle is enjoying a renaissance, particularly in the show ring. A less appreciated benefit is that properly taught, it gives stability and control and can be of real benefit to some disabled riders and to small ladies on large horses. As part of their all-round riding education, Jennie taught both Anne and Lizzie to ride side-saddle at an early stage and on her seventh birthday, Lizzie won her first ever rosette riding Dinky Toy side-saddle at the New Forest Show.

Another pony who became part of the family during those early years was Jennie's old friend and jumping partner, Polly Flinders. When Polly retired from riding she came back to Catherston and took up a new career in harness. Jennie and Anthony used to drive her to a phaeton, a light, four-wheeled buggy, and they would go off for family picnics.

Today, teaching commitments take Jennie all over the world. Inevitably, she meets the occasional rider who looks on lessons with her as a status symbol, on a par with having your hair cut at the right salon and wearing clothes with the right labels, but these are far outnumbered by those with a genuine desire to learn and progress. Teaching through the Federation Equestre Internationale (FEI) will never make her fortune, because the idea is to encourage the growth and development of dressage in countries where it has perhaps not had a traditional base, but she feels that this is her way of putting something back into the sport and way of life that has given her so much.

In the past few years Jennie has taught in countries as diverse as Australia, America, Trinidad, Barbados and Malaysia. She has met many fascinating characters, both two and four-legged, and is full of admiration for their determination and resourcefulness. She has also found a lot of talent, sometimes in places which might not seem to be the natural home of dressage, such as Malaysia.

In many ways Jennie's background makes her the ideal teacher for riders who are trying to train horses who do not fit the standard image of a dressage horse. There are some who ride imported warmbloods, but these are expensive and many of the people she meets work with ex-racehorses which they have bought off the track. Not all are working at a high level: one rider with whom she had a lot of fun was an American with a part-bred Clydesdale. He had seen her teach on a clinic and begged the organiser to let him have a lesson, which she was reluctant to do because Jennie's other pupils on that occasion were working at quite a high level.

However, when one was forced to drop out he pleaded his case again. Not quite sure how Jennie would react, the clinic organiser passed on his request; Jennie cheerfully agreed and found herself confronted by an amenable rider with a great sense of humour on a horse whose mother or father was bred to pull a plough and needed his brakes re-lined. The horse roared round the school with its head in the air, taking the corners like a motorbike, with the rider hanging on.

Not surprisingly, there were several curious spectators eager to see how one of the most famous names in international dressage would cope. They were surprised when Jennie asked if she could sit on the horse, having realised immediately that if neither he nor his rider quite understood what was happening, she would have to instill some basic understanding. Once she had helped him to understand the ABC of stop and start, which took only a short while, he proved to be perfectly willing to try his best.

Sadly, some people who have never met her before seem to expect that she will take the lesson standing on a pedestal with her nose in the air. They get a pleasant surprise when they find out that she might be Jennie Loriston-Clarke, FBHS and MBE, but she is also down to earth with a sense of humour.

7

Founder of a Dynasty

B y the beginning of 1972, Jennie was established as one of Britain's leading dressage riders and, with Kadett, was a regular member of our international teams. That year saw two huge milestones in her dressage career and also in her life – she was asked to make herself available for possible selection for the British team for the Munich Olympics and also found the horse who was to become perhaps the greatest she has ever ridden and the founder of a dynasty.

When the letter arrived asking Jennie to present herself and Kadett before the selectors, together with other candidates, she knew that winning a place on the team would be far from a walkover. At first it seemed that she would be one of the reserve riders, but then one of those selected, Jook Hall, was dealt a terrible blow. Her horse, Detective, died from colic and Jennie and the other reserves were back with a chance – though none of them would have wished it to happen that way.

The final team trial took place on 25 June and was set up in competition form, with four riders competing for two places. It was a test of nerve as well as ability and Jennie proved that she had both by coming second to her much respected mentor, Mrs Johnstone. However, although the selectors had no doubts about Jennie, they had less confidence in Kadett and felt that he was not good enough in piaffe.

Generously, Diana Mason – also on the reserve list and due to act as chef d'equipe, the all-important team leader – offered her the ride on her own horse, Pericles. Although she was used to riding difficult horses, for some reason Jennie did not get on with him. Finally, the selectors had to admit that expecting her to establish a last-minute, Olympic standard partnership with a horse she had never ridden before was over optimistic and Kadett was given his Olympic passport.

Three months later, Jennie and Anthony headed for Munich, with Anthony as lorry driver and providing much-valued moral support. Then, as always, his calm, logical approach to dealing with any problems was of enormous help, especially when Jennie was focusing on her and her horse's work-up to the competition. The British riders, along with athletes from all the other Olympic disciplines, were housed in the Olympic village and had to travel out to the Nuremberg Palace, where a dressage arena had been constructed. As Anthony was classed as a supporter and village accommodation was for competitors only, he had the less comfortable option of sleeping in the lorry.

The dressage competition was scheduled for 5 September, and Jennie did not need an alarm clock to make sure she woke up early enough. Inevitably, she was aware that she was about to ride the most important test she had faced so far, but although her adrenaline was buzzing it was from anticipation rather than fear. She knew her horse, she knew that despite the selectors' admittedly realistic reservations he deserved his chance and she wanted to get on with the job.

As she got dressed, mentally 'riding through' the test in her mind and thinking where she could gain maximum marks, there was a single loud bang from elsewhere in the village, followed by shouts and the sounds of people running around. Jennie looked out of the window, but could not see anything, and assumed that it was a problem with a vehicle backfiring. Putting the distraction to the back of her mind, she finished dressing and went to the car which took her to the palace.

Fortunately, Kadett had settled into his temporary stabling, where he was being looked after by Anthony. Getting her horse ready was an important part of the preparation for Jennie, allowing her to assess her horse's state of mind and for them both to relax into their partnership. The methodical routine of grooming, plaiting and tacking up to begin their warm-up helped her to close out any outside distractions and concentrate on what lay ahead.

As she was working on Kadett, Peter Scott Dunn, the team vet, appeared. He was obviously worried, though doing his best to present a calm exterior, and when Jennie asked what was wrong he told her that the Olympic village had become a fortress. The noise Jennie had heard earlier and attributed to a backfiring car had a far more terrifying origin: terrorists had infiltrated the village and all that was known so far was that at least one Israeli athlete had been murdered.

Later, those Games were to go down as the saddest and bloodiest in history. From then on, they were linked to what became known as the Munich Olympics massacre – an obscene and tragic waste of life by any criteria, but even more so because it was staged at the event which was meant to represent international co-operation.

Days later, the *New York Times* spelled out what was probably the most impartial and factual account of what happened. Early in the morning, eight Arab commandos broke into the village and shot two Israelis; both were team coaches, one a weight lifter and the other, a wrestler. Both died instantly. The terrorists, who Jennie later heard had been disguised as catering workers, took nine of the other eighteen members of the Israeli Olympic teams hostage and turned the village into a siege compound.

Throughout that day, West German officials tried to negotiate with the terrorists, who demanded the release of two hundred Arab guerillas being held in Israel and safe passage out of Germany for them and their hostages. Despite efforts from the Tunisian ambassador and representations from the Arab League in Bonn – and even when two West German ministers of the interior offered themselves as hostages in place of the Israelis – negotiations reached stalemate. The Israeli prime minister, Golda Meir, steadfastly refused to release any guerillas held in Israel.

The West German officials had already rejected suggestions that they should storm the compound, because it was potentially too dangerous to the hostages and the other athletes who were still in there. Eventually, two helicopters were brought in to take the terrorists and their captives out of the village to a waiting jet. Unknown to the terrorists – although they probably expected it – West German marksmen were hidden along the away. The Arabs had split their captives into two groups, and as they walked from the helicopters to the jet, someone opened fire.

Accounts as to which side fired first were confused and at the end of the day, it did not matter. What did count was the terrible death toll left in the terrorists' wake: as the first shots rang out, they immediately began shooting the Israeli hostages. The second group, which had started to leave the helicopter, threw a grenade into it, killing the remaining hostages. When the shooting finally finished, all nine Israeli hostages had been killed; five Arabs had been shot dead and three had been wounded.

When the reality of what had happened became known, Jennie, along with the rest of the world, was horrified. However, as she was preparing to go into the dressage arena, details were scarce and vague. All she could do was think about why she was there and what it meant – and through all the pressure and stress, she knew that whatever had happened, she and the other riders had to perform as well as they knew how. Somehow, there was also the feeling that by doing this, they were showing that they could not be beaten.

Both Jennie and Kadett proved that they deserved to wear the Union Jack. Mrs Johnstone, riding her test on her seventieth birthday, set the

achroyd Sololyte

standard and Jennie and Kadett followed. It was not a brilliant test, but it was the best that could have been expected from either of them in any circumstances – and better than many had dared to hope for. They finished in nineteenth place, with Kadett the second best British horse.

Later, the reality of what had happened was overwhelming. Diana Mason had come closest to it: in the early hours, someone had burst into her room and, whilst she was struggling to wake up, demanded to know if she was an Israeli. Half asleep, she answered that she was not, and by the time she was fully awake the intruder had gone.

The day became a surrealistic mix of horror, tension and exhaustion. Jennie and Anthony finally managed to get something to eat, but as she started to relax a blistering headache started to overwhelm her. At first she tried to ignore it, telling herself that it was her body's reaction to that traumatic day, but its intensity increased until eventually, she blacked out. A doctor was called and Jennie admitted that this had happened before. As there was little he could do except give her painkilling medication, the doctor said she should go home as soon as possible and have the problem investigated.

As Anthony drove her back in the lorry, her first Olympic competition seemed as if it had happened a long time ago. Although she was proud of what Kadett had achieved for her, Jennie found it hard to believe that whilst she had been riding, innocent athletes had been murdered. It did not make her performance any the less special, but it cast an ugly light on what should have been a peaceful celebration of human achievement.

The next few days went by in a blur and although she tried to get back into a normal routine, Jennie knew that something was wrong. Her own doctor could do nothing and told her that she had to go to a London hospital so that the problem could be properly investigated. Although she was reluctant, not least because she did not want to leave Anne and Lizzie, Jennie had no choice but to agree.

What started as an irritation rapidly developed into a nightmare. The treatment she received was inadequate and at first, the best they could tell her was that it might be a nerve problem. One week later, she was told that she was being sent home, but should come back a few days later to have a lumbar puncture. When she asked why, she was told, bluntly and with no attempt at farther explanation, that it was thought she might have a brain tumour.

It was a mind–chilling time, but Jennie was too numb to do more than live through those next days on automatic pilot. She remembers riding out at the weekend and thinking here I am, at thirty-three and with two little daughters, and this is what might be happening to me. If the worst scenario turned out to be reality, what would happen to the girls and to Anthony? And, of course, because her mother had died from cancer there was the awful fear that the same thing was happening to her.

Somehow, the waiting period went by and Jennie went back to hospital. The one good thing was that although the lumbar puncture was unpleasant, the result of that and other tests showed that there was no tumour. The reason for the pain and the blackouts was that her neck was out of joint: in itself, that was good news, but the bad news was that the doctors told her she would just have to live with the problem. The most they could tell her was that she would be all right sometimes and not all right at others - and, as an offshoot, that she might have to surrender her driving licence.

Jennie discovered that the headaches occurred because the arteries in her neck were being pinched. When she felt uncomfortable, she held her neck stiffly without being aware of it, restricting the blood flow, and when she relaxed, the sudden restoration of blood flow caused the pain. She lived with this knowledge, and irregular episodes of pain, until one day it became too much to bear.

She remembers waking up one morning and being unable to get out of bed – all she could do was roll over on to her side. Half in desperation and half out of the logic of knowing that there is more than one solution to any problem, Jennie decided that she would find a good chiropractor. She had the good fortune to choose Dr Faye, a Canadian chiropractor in Southampton, who immediately X-rayed her spine. As soon as he had the plates, he was able to show Jennie that the only surprising thing about the devastating pain and consequential blackouts she had suffered for so long was that she had managed to put up with it for so long.

Her neck was completely out of alignment, a legacy of the whiplash injury she had suffered when riding Wayfarer. To literally add insult to injury, her GP had noticed that her specialist had noted this, but thought it was of no consequence. Manipulation by Dr Faye enabled the muscles attached to the vertebrae to realign them and the results were, to Jennie, a miracle. Since then she has had no major problems, though she knows that if her neck is put under stress – perhaps because a young or exuberant horse yanks at the rein whilst being lunged – she has to watch out for the tell tale signs of headaches. If that happens, she goes back to the chiropractor for assessment and if necessary, treatment.

Her own experiences have made her aware that horses, too, suffer from back and neck pain; unlike their riders, they are unable to explain this and can only show it through behaviour such as resistance, rearing or bucking. Over the years many people have sent young and difficult horses to Catherston for backing and schooling and the first task is always to assess their conformation, musculature and movement. If a horse has a reputation for bucking but has muscles which are more developed on one side of its hindquarters than the other, Jennie knows that most probably it has or has had a physical problem. If you are a horse and it hurts when someone rides you, there are only so many ways you can show this – but, sadly, there are many riders who cannot see beyond the 'give it a whack' approach.

When Kadett came back from the Olympics, Jennie decided to rest him for the winter. The strength of competition in Munich had also shown that whilst he had done his best for her and would always be special, she and his owner, Mrs Steele, had to accept that he was not going to win medals. Mrs Steele was as keen as Jennie to find a horse with that elusive star quality and it was decided that they would look for a youngster to bring on and eventually take over from Kadett.

Jennie was impressed by the paces, conformation and temperaments of the Dutch warmbloods, who at that time were lighter, more elegant and seemed more intelligent than German breeds such as the Hanoverian. She explains that whilst a dressage horse has to be trainable, it needs to have a genuine enthusiasm for its work that expresses itself in presence, lightness and power, not be an obedient but dull automaton. Fashions and demands change and today's riders want what Jennie was looking for in the 1970s: at that time, though, many Hanoverians were powerful but lacked the grace and elegance that to Jennie was synonymous with dressage at its best. Later the lines were to be given greater infusions of Thoroughbred blood, and as another British rider puts it, became less like dancing elephants.

Buying a dressage horse in Europe today means becoming part of a slick, efficient and costly marketing exercise. Sadly, most riders seeking top prospects still go abroad to buy, though over the years Catherston's bloodlines became so well known and so successful that they found themselves doing the equestrian equivalent of selling coals to Newcastle. Many Catherston horses have been exported and are flying the British flag abroad, particularly in America, but until recently Britain has not been able to even start to compete with the sales machinery of performance sales such as Verden in Germany. These are organised so that breeders of Hanoverian sport horses can sell their stock from foals to elite sport horses. The auctions for elite horses, first organised in 1949, are held twice a year and attract buyers and big prices from all over the world.

When Mrs Steele and Jennie decided that the latter should go horse hunting, the business was much more easy going and relaxed. She looked at many horses in Britain but could not find anything that met all her demands, and after competing on Kadett at Frankfurt Show took the opportunity to break the journey home and stop off in Holland to go shopping.

Her guide once again was Rocky, who used to train in Holland and knew many of the Dutch breeders. Jennie was thinking not only in competition terms, but also of strengthening Catherston's breeding policies, and wanted either a stallion or a mare. They were told of various so-called outstanding prospects, but all these were rejected for one reason or another. One farm in the south of Holland offered a mare that Jennie did not like, but she caught a fleeting glimpse of an intelli-gent-looking head over another door and wandered over to look. Inside the stable was a gangly colt who, though she could not assess his movement or even his conformation properly, looked at her with a mixture of curiosity and boldness that instantly appealed to her.

Rocky asked if they could have a look at him, but the owner of the farm was ill in bed with flu and his wife muttered that this was impossible – she could not take the horse out of his box without him being there. As there was nothing they could do, Jennie and Rocky called it a day and went on to the other farms on their list.

The results were similarly discouraging. The horses they were shown were either too big and heavy or too light, or had conformation which meant that even with careful training they would find it very difficult to perform advanced movements such as passage and piaffe. Jennie was by then fed up and dispirited, and they were running out of time.

As they prepared to make their way home, she had a nagging recollection in the back of her mind of the colt they had seen earlier. Logic told her that if the owner's wife was unwilling or frightened to show him off, there could be a problem – perhaps he had a doubtful temperament, or even a soundness problem. But knowing that if she did not do something about it, she would be kicking herself all the way home, Jennie persuaded Rocky to go back for a second look.

Their welcome was just as discouraging as it had been first time round, but Rocky, never one to back off a challenge, would not accept no. He went to the house and literally dragged the poor owner from his bed, ignoring his wife's protestations that he could not be disturbed. The man seemed quite surprised that they wanted to see the colt, but realised that it would be easier to give in to Rocky's insistence than to try and dissuade them.

As the colt came out of the box, Jennie's first impression was that he looked like a racehorse. Lean, relatively narrow and barely 15.3hh, he reminded her of a smaller version of Anneli Drummond-Hay's Badminton winner Merely a Monarch, who was later an equally successful show jumper. The owner, now resigned to their eccentricity, explained that the colt had failed the grading tests as a potential stallion and was to be gelded.

Jennie asked to see the horse trotted up, and as soon as she saw him move felt the first stirrings of excitement: that unmistakable tingle anyone who has ever looked for a horse and thought 'This is the one' will recognise. The little bay had so much presence and élan that he looked much bigger, and as he was turned to trot back towards Jennie and Rocky, snow began to fall. The colt, barely three years old, lowered his quarters and lengthened his stride in a way that made Jennie feel that perhaps he could answer all her questions.

Logic told her that even if she was wrong and he did not make a dressage horse, he would make a lovely stallion for Catherston. The only other stallion she had at the time was the Thoroughbred, Xenocles, and this colt would make a good outcross. They went home saying that they would buy him at the right money, and Jennie left Rocky to negotiate on the asking price, which was the equivalent of £1000.

Jennie had just sold a pony to Holland, so arranged for the transporter to turn around and pick up the new colt. As yet no money had changed hands, and unimpressed by Jennie and Rocky's unblemished reputations, the vendor refused to let the horse go until he had seen the colour of her cash. The phone lines between England and Holland turned red hot with furious negotiations, until with the price agreed at around £750, the farmer agreed to put the colt on the lorry if they would guarantee the money.

Today, £750 sounds a ludicrously small amount, for which you would buy nothing more than an average small pony. Even then it was not expensive, but as far as the farmer was concerned he had a failed and probably extremely feisty stallion that he would have to geld and sell as – in his eyes – a second-rate horse. Although Jennie had the gut feeling that the colt could be special, she knew she was taking a gamble; even she could not have dreamed just how special he would become. Somewhere in Holland, there may still be a farmer who talks about the day he let one of the world's top dressage stallions slip through his fingers.

Peden, the transport company that was later to be owned and run by Jennie's brother Mike Bullen, brought the colt back to Catherston. As the lorry pulled up at Catherston and Jennie went out to greet it, the driver grinned at her. She remembers his exact words: 'You've got a wild one here' – and that they were nearly drowned out by a furious scream from the box's occupant.

With a mixture of anticipation and trepidation on Jennie's part, they lowered the ramp. The little colt, his coat dark with sweat, glared at her from the top of it and screamed out an announcement of his arrival. Jennie says that it was as if on the journey over he had worked himself into a cocktail of excitement that was about to explode, but at the same time she could not but admire the fabulous head and the bold eyes that blazed out in indignation.

'I'll need some Dutch Courage to ride this one,' she thought to herself – and a split second later, knew she had given the colt his new name. He was to become affectionately known at home as Bill, after Jennie's pet name for Charlie; for no particular reason, but simply because it seemed fun at the time, she nicknamed him Bill whilst he labelled her as Fred! 'Bill from Groningen' somehow seemed appropriate, but as Dutch Courage he was to write himself and his rider into the record books. That furious little colt, no matter how unlikely it would have seemed at the time, was to become a legend in the dressage world and the founder of a dynasty.

Once he had settled in his new home, he was not as wild and bolshie as Jennie's first impressions led her to expect. Bill was intelligent and would not have suffered fools gladly, but showed a willingness to learn and to work… when she could keep his attention. As far as she knew, he had only been sat on four or five times before she bought him, so it was a case of starting from scratch and establishing a relationship. With hindsight, she was glad that she had the chance to start with an almost blank sheet, because the old adage that you tell a gelding, ask a mare and discuss it with a stallion proved to be true. Bill proved himself open to discussion, but there were times when Jennie had to point out that they had actually had this particular discussion before and he had agreed to her terms.

One of her first concerns was how on earth she was going to cope with this curious, vociferous creature in the New Forest, with all the mares and foals wandering about. A lesser rider would have taken the easier way out and not tried at all – but then, as now, Jennie expected her stallions to behave in a civilised way so that they could enjoy an interesting and varied life.

Once she had established basic control in the school and knew that she could stop, start and steer, Jennie started hacking out with Bill in the forest. At first she rode him near, but not too close to, mares and foals, who were far less interested in him than he was in them. When he neighed, trying to show them what an impressive person he was, she told him off; not by hitting him or trying to bully him, simply by scolding him with her voice and riding him forwards. For such an intelligent, sensitive horse, this was enough and he soon learned that when he was being ridden, he gave his full attention to his work.

There are competitors in all spheres who restrict stallions to the confines of an arena and only take them into other environments when they compete them, but Jennie feels that this is counter productive and unfair. Her attitude has always been that if you treat a stallion as a normal horse, within the boundaries of safety and mutual respect, he will behave like one. Conversely, if you treat him like a wild animal, that is what you are likely to end up with.

Nearly thirty years later, that philosophy – to Jennie's amusement and surprise – was to send a ripple of disbelief through the horse world. The cause was a photograph in *Horse & Hound* of three Catherston stallions cantering side by side along a grassy gallop at the stud, ears pricked and obviously enjoying every moment. Their riders, who include Jennie and Lizzie, are perfectly in control and the stallions are focused on them, not on each other.

When Catherston is at its fullest capacity, walking into the stallion barn is an awesome experience. The occupants range from Dutch Courage's sons, grandsons and great grandsons to those from other bloodlines whose owners have asked Jennie to stand them at the stud. Notable 'outsiders' have included Liboi and the Queen's Sanbal, both lovely Thoroughbreds. Rock King, the leading international eventing stallion co-owned by Charlie Bullen's wife, Sarah, was another much sought after stallion, but sadly had to be put down after shattering his pelvis after a fall at Tweseldown in 2000.

It was one of those freak accidents that upset everyone in the family. Rock King, known at home as Blanco, had a wonderful temperament and has left a legacy of talented offspring. He also had a serious amount of ability, and when he died, at the age of ten, had 247 eventing points. Jennie says that it was one of those unbelievable accidents: he seemed to just touch a fence with his knee, then flipped over.

Even when the greatest care is taken, accidents will happen – and as Jennie knows, it is always heartbreaking. Catherston Dambuster, a young stallion destined for stardom, slipped whilst walking across the yard and damaged his hock so badly he had to be put down. He was only nine years old, but was already established as a Grand Prix horse with Jennie and had a brilliant future ahead of him. More recently, a Catherston-bred Thoroughbred by Jennie and Anthony's Delta Dancer was broken at the stud and went into training as a three-year-old. She was sent out with the string and cantered well, then on the way back to the yard her back end seized up. Thinking it was a condition called azoturia, which causes severe muscle cramping, the girl riding her jumped off. When the vet arrived, it was discovered that somehow, the filly had fractured her pelvis – and though she may be able to be used for breeding, she will never get to the racecourse.

The first thing any visitor to Catherston notices, whether or not he or she knows anything about stallions, is that as soon as you walk into the stallion barn you are greeted by two rows of interested, friendly heads with pricked ears. There are no grumpy faces and certainly no attempts at aggression; any stallion that showed the slightest signs would have found his anatomy and his breeding prospects cut abruptly short! It is fascinating to see how they all recognise Jennie and you can almost see them thinking 'Oh good, it's the boss'. The ones with whom she has a special bond are even more amazing; Dutch Gold performs piaffe in his box because he thinks it will please her, then turns round as if to say 'That's what you wanted, isn't it?'

Catherston stallions know that when they are tacked up with a saddle and bridle, they are expected to work and to put other matters out of their minds. When the covering bridle – one used to lead the stallion to a waiting mare – goes on, they know the difference but are still expected to behave like gentlemen! As the lucky stallion is brought out, the others will whinny softly as if to acknowledge that it is his turn for a romantic encounter.

Jennie prefers not to cover with a stallion until he has learned the basic work ethics and accepts tactful discipline from a rider; raging hormones coupled with a lack of education spell disaster. Bill therefore did nothing else whilst he was at nursery school, and once the basics were in place Jennie decided to turn him away to relax and mature in the company of Our Nobby. At first, the plan was to rest him until he was four, but Our Nobby managed to strain his hock out in the field, probably through over-exuberant play.

As a result, both horses were brought back in. Jennie felt that because Bill was in the latter part of his third year, she might as well ride him a little more and start competing him as a four-year-old. He took to his renewed lessons with enthusiasm, as an intelligent horse will often do if he has an equally intelligent rider who can make the lessons enjoyable. Bill was still impetuous, but the more he worked, the better he became and the more he enjoyed himself. Like an intelligent child, he liked to be kept interested and enjoyed doing different things, from working in the school to hacking in the forest.

8

Star Performers

As a four-year-old, Dutch Courage was still more of an equine Clark Kent than the Superman he was to become. Relatively small and lightweight, he was nevertheless intelligent and enjoyed his work; if he had been a child, he would have been one of those who thrive on challenges. Looking at all he achieved later, it would be natural to assume that he burst on the competitive scene with fanfares and accolades, but the reality was much more low key. His competition debut was uninspiring and no one really took much notice of him beyond the fact that he was Jennie's new novice.

He did win a couple of third placings and at that stage, Jennie was content. She never wavered in her conviction that her skinny little duckling would one day be a powerful swan, but, outside the family, kept her thoughts to herself. If ever doubts did creep in, she consoled herself with the fact that at the very least, she had a good potential stallion. It was tempting to use him and see what his first offspring would be like, but because Bill was still rather volatile Jennie decided that he needed to concentrate on work, not mares!

In the end, he had little chance to give his attention to either. Somehow, Bill injured his shoulder and had to be box rested; it was frustrating for Jennie, because she wanted to work him, but a lifetime with horses had taught her that there are times when all you can do is wait. Box rest, where a horse is confined to its stable to limit movement and allow injuries to heal, can be a nightmare. By nature,

Right: Richard Meade on Leamington Pavlova and Jennie on Mystic Rights at the Horse of the Year Show when they won the hack pairs (*Monty*)

Below: With the legendary Colonel Sir Mike Ansell (*right*) receiving the Sherry Shippers' Award for the most stunning performance at the Horse of the Year Show. Jennie won the award with Kadett (*Leslie Lane*)

Dutch Courage winning the Grand Prix at Solihull, 1977

Above: 1978 Goodwood World Championships. Gold medal winner Christine Stuckelberger with Granat (*centre*), Uwe Schulten-Baumer with Slipowitz (silver) and Jennie with Dutch Courage, bronze medal winners (*Kit Houghton*)

Below: Dutch Courage and Jennie hacking out at home with constant companion Foxy (*Kit Houghton*)

Dutch Courage takes a keen interest in Cleopatra at Goodwood. This was in 1980, the year they won every class

Horse of the Year Show, 1982. Dutch Courage enjoying himself in the lime-
light although he never liked the preliminary rounds (*Kit Houghton*)

Long reining demonstration with Dutch Courage at Gatcombe. Jennie is wearing her 'lucky' red, white and blue Jubilee socks (*Kit Houghton*)

Jennie and Prince Consort at the 1984 Olympics. Jennie had only ridden him for ten days before the Olympics

Dutch Gold competing at Locko Park (*above*) over the third fence (*Kit Houghton*) and (*below*) over the fifteenth fence

horses need liberty: in the wild, they will cover fifteen miles a day looking for food, so shutting them up in a stable, however large and luxurious, for long periods can be the same as imprisoning them.

Fortunately, Bill's temperament was such that he accepted his confinement with as good grace as could be expected. Jennie made sure that he had plenty of attention and plenty to look at, and by providing a constant supply of hay was able to mimic the grazing behaviour essential for a horse's mental as well as physical health. Even so, it was a case of hoping and praying when she was told she could introduce light exercise again, as so often a horse will explode at his first taste of being outside his four walls once more and possibly hurt himself again.

Bill must either have had a natural sense of self preservation or decided that starting work was more fun than standing in his stable. Over a period of weeks, Jennie brought him back to where they had left off and gradually began to ask a little more. As he lost his babyishness and started to be able to concentrate for longer periods, so he started to fill out and grow. Correct work coupled with correct feeding transformed him that winter, and by the time he reached his fifth summer the racehorse-like 15.3hh colt was a 16.1hh stallion.

Those who saw him in his heyday always thought he was much bigger, but this was down to star quality. Just as Mel Gibson gives the impression of being a six footer, so Dutch Courage could give the impression that he was 17hh. He managed to combine powerful paces with the elegance and neatness of a smaller horse and as a result, his training advanced at a rate most riders would find incredible. Jennie was careful always to give him enough of a challenge to enjoy, but never to push him too hard, too soon – though when your five-year-old finds flying changes a total doddle, it must make you wonder if you have a child prodigy on your hands!

Even at that stage, Jennie and Dutch Courage was a partnership that was meant to be. Her approach to work was exactly what he needed, because it was always interesting and fun for him. Like so many of his children, he delighted in learning new things and had such enormous natural athleticism that he could have done anything; Jennie's interest was dressage, but Dutch Courage could equally as well have gone show jumping or eventing. It was all there in his bloodlines as well as his natural conformation and movement – he was a three-quarters brother to Laramie, who won the show jumping Grand Prix at Olympia, and half brother to Jumbo Design, who was on the Dutch show jumping team at the Montreal Olympics.

These days, even riders who are not interested in dressage as a competitive sport often have an appreciation of it. Common sense dictates that a horse which is balanced and obedient is more pleasant to ride than one that is on its forehand and unruly, and whilst they may take a different approach from 'pure' dressage trainers, successful show jumpers probably spend more time working on the flat than they do over fences. As one leading trainer puts it, it isn't the fences that count but the bits in between them.

In the 1970s, that message was starting to get through even if there was still a school of opinion that the only reason anyone would choose to do dressage was because he or she was too frightened to jump. There was also a feeling in some quarters that top level dressage was to some extent, circus tricks – that movements such as piaffe and passage were artificial. As Jennie points out, the truth of the matter is that all the movements she trains her horses to perform are ones they could, if they chose to, perform naturally out in the field.

Catherston horses, because they are bred to be athletes, find it easier than some to carry out demanding movements such as piaffe, passage and canter pirouettes. But watch the commonest, hairiest cob on a frosty or windy day when something spooks him and you might well see him offer steps of passage. The horse can do it on his own: it is the rider who has to learn how to teach him and help him to do it on request and with the added burden of a human being on his back.

Later on in Dutch Courage's fifth year, Rocky came to Catherston to catch up on Dutch Courage's progress and help Jennie with his training. He was so pleased with the way the young stallion had come on that he told Jennie he felt he was ready to start piaffe. Jennie asked him to show her how this was taught at the Spanish Riding School, where he had spent so many years. In Vienna, the young stallions are introduced to this and other advanced movements on long reins, with a trainer on the ground encouraging them to flex their hocks by gently tapping with a long whip. Success depends on the trainer's knowledge and ability to apply the aids with split second timing, and Rocky has long been acknowledged as a master of in-hand work.

Dutch Courage decided that whatever the Spanish Riding School Lipizzaners could do, he could do better. Within two days, he had picked it up; within three, he had it off to a fine art. Jennie says that different horses have different talents and some can perform passage to a high level but find piaffe much more difficult. In passage, the horse moves forwards in a very slow, elevated trot; in piaffe, which is the ultimate in trot collection, the horse stays on the spot throughout. Passage is usually easier because the horse has his forward motion to help him, but Bill found it more difficult.

As Bill approached the end of his fifth year, Jennie knew that he was the best horse she had ever had. He was so supple, so athletic and so intelligent that nothing was a problem for him. However, this would not have been the case if he had been in the hands of a less knowledgeable rider or, even worse, one who had tried to force instead of persuade. Jennie used the same approach with Bill that she employed with her daughters – she said 'Don't you think it would be fun if we did this?' In all three cases, as at least Anne and Lizzie will confirm, it worked.

Although she did not do much jumping with Bill, they used to pop over small logs and streams whilst hacking in the forest. Jennie soon learned that the power that made Bill's piaffe so good was equally in evidence here, as he would jump four feet over a tiny stream. Later, his progeny were to show the same attitude and ability; he was not only the leading sire of dressage horses and show jumpers but the third highest sire in the table of eventing sires.

It is tempting to think that we could all train horses to the same level as Dutch Courage and his children if only we had horses of the same ability. But Jennie's ability as a trainer owes so much to her under-standing of the way horses think and react that she could – and often has – trained the most unlikely animals to do the most unlikely things. She says she owes much of this to the attitudes and methods she absorbed from her parents, who taught her that if a horse found a task difficult you had to find a way of making it easier for him.

Both those who insist on sanctifying dressage and those who disparage it as 'circus tricks' would be surprised to know that Jennie used to go to Bertram Mills' circus and was fascinated by what she saw. One trainer in particular, called Alex Kerr, influenced her through his approach to the lions and tigers he worked with and through his book, *No Bars Between* (Cassell 1957). Its title came about because he trained and worked his animals loose, with no safety bars and without sticks or whips.

One of his golden rules, which Jennie absorbed and followed with her stallions, was that you had to gain these big cats' attention and respect in equal measures: a rule that the animals themselves lived by. Failing to do this meant putting your life at risk, as one of his panthers discovered. Every time it walked past a particular lion, the panther would dab at its head with its paw, until eventually the lion had a sore ear. The day came when the lion had simply had enough, and swiped back in retaliation with a blow so forceful the panther was killed instantly.

Alex Kerr, a former RAF officer, was a master of the classic crowd pleasers and would fearlessly put his head in a lion's mouth. During one performance, the crowd made so much noise whilst he was doing this that the lion began to panic. Mr Kerr related that he knew there was only one thing he could do, and it was the hardest challenge he had ever faced: somehow, he had to stay relaxed so that the big cat did not pick up on his fear.

During those few, seemingly interminable seconds the crowd had no idea what was happening, but his nerve held and he emerged unscathed. It was the worst and bravest moment of his career as a trainer, and also signalled the end of it. The ordeal that had tested his nerve to the utmost had also broken it; he never performed that act again, though carried on training animals until he retired a short time afterwards.

To this day, Jennie would probably rather put her head in a lion's mouth than walk into a roomful of strangers, though she has become so good at overcoming her fear that few would realise what an ordeal it represents. However, the inspiration provided by Mr Kerr, coupled with her childhood lessons and natural gift for lateral thinking, mean that she

has quietly been practising the 'natural horsemanship' that the equestrian world has adopted with such enthusiasm over the past few years.
From Catherston's point of view, and without disparaging the trainers
who have done so much to increase understanding of horse psychology,
much of it has been a case of re-inventing the wheel.

As a young man, Colonel Bullen trained at an Italian cavalry school
where feats such as riding down precipices were part of normal training.
It was legendary in the family that the Bullens were wild horsemen;
Henry Bullen once won a wager by jumping his horse over a river.
Anne Bullen was always fascinated by training and before Jennie was
born, had her own circus in conjunction with her sister, the artist
Rosamund Oldfield. Rosamund trained dogs and Anne concentrated on
ponies, and between them they built up quite a following.

One of Anne's star performers was a pony called Darkie, a little
Dartmoor who she had rescued from being kept in a chicken hut. He
learned to count, and to 'go to bed,' lying down and pulling the blanket
over himself. She also trained the Marshwood Shetland ponies, who
were bred and owned by a family friend called Betty Cox, to perform
feats such as jumping over picnic tables, complete with place settings
and picnic.

Welsh Pony

As children, Jennie, Jane and Sarah gained as much fun from training ponies as from riding them. Jennie taught Double Bubble, the palomino son of Bubbly, to lie down on command so that her daughters could both sit on him at the same time. This was done first by holding up a front leg for gradually longer periods, then strapping it up, giving a verbal command and tapping him on the knee. As soon as he showed a glimmer of understanding, he would be praised and rewarded.

Jennie says that as long as you teach them in a safe, logical manner, horses and ponies love learning. Teaching your pony to lie down may sound as if it should carry a 'Don't do this at home' warning, but precautions were always taken so there was no risk of an animal hurting itself. Word soon spread that if you wanted a pony you could trust under any circumstances, you went to the Bullen family – and that word eventually reached the highest quarters.

When the Dartmoor Pony Society wanted to present a pony to the young Prince Charles, it was important that it should not only be an excellent specimen of the breed but that it should be as safe as possible. As a result, Juniper, a pretty little four-year-old, arrived at Catherston. Within a few months he was used to the Bullen girls crawling between his legs and sliding off his tail and would even stand like a rock whilst they rested a ladder against his backside and climbed up it on to his back.

Although Jennie never set out to capitalise on her more unusual training skills, her reputation as the woman who could train any horse to do anything prompted some unusual interludes at Catherston. When Lloyds Bank wanted to capitalise on its logo, which featured a rearing black horse, the creative powers-that-be wanted the real thing.

They entrusted the search to a company called Intellectual Animals, who approached Jennie because of Catherston's reputation for breeding and training quality horses. Her brief was to train a black horse to canter round the forest so it could be filmed running free with flowing mane and tail, then rear on command to imitate the logo. The first horse she used was a Trakehner called Kustos, who was owned by Mrs Tee – better known as the owner of the international show jumper Tee's Hanauer.

Kustos had all the looks but, unfortunately, lacked the necessary boldness; Jennie taught him to rear, but he was reluctant to gallop behind a camera car. Getting him to canter down the track in the first place had called on Jennie's ingenuity: she had to find a way of regulating his speed and making sure he did not duck out to the side. Jennie decided that the obvious way to hold his attention was to ride a mare in front. Over the years, she has found that most stallions are attracted to grey mares – perhaps it is the equine equivalent of 'gentlemen prefer blondes' – but when one was provided, Kustos declined to be tempted. However, when a chestnut New Forest stallion was substituted, he perked up and had no hesitation in seeing off the interloper.

The camera car, however, was a different proposition. As all the best hearthrobs in the film world have their stunt doubles, Jennie decided that this would have to be the answer here – and she knew that Catherston Nightsafe could be just the four-legged star she needed. A grandson of Bubbly, Nightsafe was only 13.2hh but his conformation and movement were so superb that Jennie knew that on camera, no one would be able to tell the difference. Nightsafe had a lovely temperament and although officially bay, was so dark that no one could quibble. In any case, Jennie's experience in producing horses for the show ring meant that there were plenty of ways of enhancing the few brown hairs, if necessary.

Her first step was to teach him to rear, just as she had with Kustos. Rearing is natural behaviour for a stallion: when rivals meet in the wild, they stand on their hindlegs to try and intimidate each other and strike out with their forelegs. Teaching a horse and particularly a stallion to rear on command is therefore not something to enter into lightly, but Nightsafe had inherited his grandsire's amazing temperament and Jennie knew that he respected her and would not try and shift the balance of power.

As with all training, this was accomplished through pleasure and reward, not intimidation. Jennie started by holding a titbit just out of reach, then tapped him on his knees and gave the verbal command 'Up'. Nightsafe's reaction was to give a little bounce off his front legs, so she immediately praised him and gave him his reward. Once he had the idea, it was simply a case of encouraging him to react to the voice command alone and to go higher each time. Within days, he was rearing in a style that Champion the Wonder Horse would have envied.

The next challenge was to get Nightsafe to follow the camera car without wearing any visible tack, because the advertising agency wanted romantic shots suggesting speed and freedom. After some experimenting, Jennie equipped Nightsafe with a roller – a padded strap which fastened round his middle – and made a long, thin braided rope from fishing lines. By fastening one end of the fishing line rope to the roller and holding on to the other as she hung out of the back of the film car, she was able to keep contact with the stallion. He was so responsive to her voice that she could speed him up or slow him down by verbal commands, and the angle of the camera shots means that neither the transparent rope nor the roller showed up on film.

Nightsafe performed beautifully. To this day, few people realise that the double for Kustos, who stood 16 hands, was a 13.2hh pony... and that as he thunders along the forest track, ears pricked and mane flowing, Jennie is leaning out of the film car holding on to a fishing line.

The final headache was to provide Kustos, who ended up sharing the role with Nightsafe, with a long, flowing mane. As his was about four inches long and neatly pulled, and there was no time to let it grow, the only answer was to create a false one. Lengths of black hair were pulled from a selection of other horses and Jennie carefully wove them into Kustos's own mane – rather like the hair extensions for which exclusive salons charge a small fortune. The result was flowing locks authentic enough to satisfy the most demanding art director.

To be a top competitor in any field, you have to be dedicated and single minded. However, single mindedness is not necessarily synonymous with tunnel vision and Jennie has always believed that any horse or pony, of any type, can be trained to perform to a good standard. Just as important, training and performing must be fun for horse and rider.

Jennie enjoyed organising musical rides: entertaining displays where teams of horses or ponies performed routines to music. To be successful, these rely on teamwork and accuracy, especially when the animals taking part were of widely differing types. It only takes one rider to go the wrong way for a carefully choreographed ride to fall into chaos.

Almost without realising it, Jennie earned the reputation of being a theatrical genius. In the late 1970s, the National Pony Society asked her if she would organise a quadrille at the Royal International Horse Show to demonstrate the versatility of Britain's native ponies; as a lifelong enthusiast, particularly of Welsh Cobs, she agreed. It was to be an enjoyable challenge and a mammoth headache at the same time: most quadrilles comprise horses which match in terms of size, type and stride length to give uniformity of appearance and ease of choreography, but Jennie's native quadrille went from one extreme to the other!

British natives share the common denominators of being tough, hardy and beautiful, but that is as far as the similarities between them go. They range from the tiny Shetland, which stands under thirty-six inches and at full speed looks like a flying ball of hair on blurred legs, to the Welsh Cob, which averages 14.2hh to 15.1hh and has an extended trot that only a few handlers can keep up with. In between are breeds such as the Highland, bred to carry shot stags weighing fourteen stone down from the Scottish hills, and the Connemara and New Forest, riding ponies which can carry children or adults.

The ponies and their riders, selected by the NPS as ambassadors of the various breeds, came from all over the country and Jennie had only three days in which to work with them. Planning and choreography took a great deal of thought, because the ponies had such different lengths of stride. The hardest thing of all was to persuade the Welsh Cobs to canter slowly – the Shetlands were quite happy to speed up, but it was essential that everyone stayed in control.

Appearances were vital and everything and everyone had to be spotless, from gleaming coats on the ponies to gleaming boots for the riders. On the big night, it was announced suddenly that the show was running ahead of schedule and the quadrille riders had to be ready to go on early. One of the last tasks was to paint the ponies' hooves with special hoof oil to make them black and shiny, and somehow one of the helpers kicked over a tin of oil with a brush laying on top of it.

Unfortunately, the oil splattered all over a dazzling white Welsh pony and his rider so that with just a few minutes to go, Jennie was presented with a white pony and child, both covered with black spots. The only answer was to scrub them both down and send them in; the pony was still wet, but under the lights, no one realised.

The Welsh Cob quadrille at Olympia, held at Christmas and perhaps the ultimate show in terms of family entertainment, was another of Jennie's triumphs and highlighted the many talents of the breed. First the twelve cobs performed a musical ride; then some were driven, followed by a spectacular activity ride finale which included jumping through fire. Like all animals, horses are naturally terrified of fire and to persuade one to jump under a blazing hoop calls for enormous trust between horse and rider.

The Metropolitan Police lent Jennie their equipment to train the fire jumpers, and told her it would probably take six weeks before the cobs were confident. Even then, she was warned, some horses could never be persuaded. Jennie only had a few days, but had such confidence in her team that she was sure it could be done. One of the strongest partnerships was that of Lizzie and the dun Bryn-y-Mor Comet, owned by John and Mary Holmes. He was successful in driving, dressage, show jumping and eventing, first with Anne and later with Lizzie.

One of the keys to successful training is to break down your eventual aim into easier tasks, rather like stepping stones. Once the ponies were happily jumping down a line of small brush fences, placed one stride apart, Jennie added the hoops that would eventually be set on fire and got them used to jumping underneath them. This caused no problems, so it was time to introduce the real thing.

The hoops were coated with special flammable string, and to everyone's delight the Welsh Cobs showed no signs of fear. As the first attempt had gone so well, Jennie instructed them to come round again. This time, disaster struck. As Lizzie and Comet bounded over the brush fence, the hoop slipped and came down on top of them. By a miracle, the top had not caught fully alight and Lizzie's quick reactions enabled her to push it off and away with no harm done.

Although she had never been so terrified, Jennie remembered the advice her mother had so often given her: whatever happens, don't show surprise or fear. Somehow she managed to stay calm; the hoop was securely replaced and relit and she told Lizzie to come round again straight away. As if nothing had happened, she and Comet cantered back and over the fence as if the blazing hoop was not there.

Catherston still finds itself the focus for unusual requests. Two years ago one of the big confectionery companies ran a competition inviting purchasers to write in with their dreams and perhaps see them come true. One lady wrote an entry which many horse lovers will appreciate: she dreamed of seeing a handsome prince ride to her door on a handsome white stallion, when she would send the prince packing and keep the horse! It was good enough to win her a lovely young Lusitano, but to make sure that the horse and his new owner got off to a good start, he was sent to Catherston to be broken in.

9

Working in Partnership

Dutch Courage might have had an uninspiring start as a four-year-old, but over the next two years he more than made up for it. As a five-year-old, he came second in the National Championships at Medium level, impressing the judges with his lightness and balance. He found even the more advanced work easy and as Jennie worked with him, she knew that she had found the best horse she had ever ridden. A lot of other people began to think the same, and at the age of six, Bill was competing at Advanced level. He made his international debut on the small tour – the inner satellite of the top international shows – and attracted great interest from international riders and trainers at Aachen.

Bill had proved that he had everything needed to be a top class sire as well as a top class performer – breeding, ability, soundness and an exceptional temperament – and Jennie decided that it was time for him to cover his first mares. At that time the only way foals were produced was the way Nature intended, though ten years later Catherston started a pilot scheme of artificial insemination. Although she thought his temperament would stand up to the dual demands of riding and covering, it was still a nerve racking time.

When Bill's hormones kicked in, would he continue to accept Jennie as 'the boss'? Just as important, would he stand up mentally to the pressures of competition, when at times he might be expected to work alongside mares in season and other stallions? Then, as now, there might be the occasional rider whose gamesmanship plans included deliberately 'winding up' a stallion in the hope that it would adversely affect its performance.

Fortunately, Bill accepted both sex and schooling with enjoyment. His first mares were proven brood mares and soon Jennie was in the exciting position of waiting for his first offspring to be born. Next year, 1976, was to prove even more memorable, though she did not know it at the time. Bill was introduced to a mare called Gold K and the result was a colt foal called Dutch Gold, who was to become the other really great horse of Jennie's career. Bill was already founding a dynasty.

By this time, the British horse world was very slowly waking up to the attraction and value of dressage, both as a discipline in its own right and an essential tool in the development of every horse, whatever its ultimate role in life. After all, the translation of dressage is, quite simply, training. Goodwood, the wonderful home of the Duke and Duchess of Richmond and Gordon on the edge of the Sussex Downs, became the centre of competition for British dressage and an important international venue for twenty-one years – as the late Dr Reiner Klimke, one of the greatest riders and trainers of all times, told Jane Kidd in her book *Goodwood Dressage Champions* (Threshold Books): 'Without Goodwood, you would not have dressage in Britain'.

In 1976 it was the venue for the international championships, which reinforced the supremacy of the German riders, led by Harry Boldt. The British Dressage Group used it as an Olympic trial for prospective team members, who included Jennie and Kadett. She knew that Kadett could never match Dutch Courage, but at that time Bill was not ready to compete at that level; Kadett had done his best for her in Munich and she could only hope that he would do so again in Montreal. Interest in and press coverage of Goodwood was therefore more intense than usual and though Germany's supremacy could not be denied – Harry Boldt won the Grand Prix on Cosima and compatriot Hans-Dietmar Wolff was second on Renommee – one of *Horse & Hound's* most influential columnists, who had seen Jennie's entertaining displays of dressage at Wembley, was not impressed.

Dorian Williams, who wrote for many years under the name of Loriner and whose identity was kept secret until his death, commented that many of the riders and horses looked stilted. 'Dressage, surely, should be relaxed and flowing,' he wrote. 'These were the qualities that made Jennie Loriston-Clarke's displays at Wembley such a delight.'

The team for Montreal was announced as Diana Mason – who was also chairman of the dressage group – and Special Edition, Sarah Whitmore and Junker and Jennie and Kadett. It was a long journey and any hopes that it might take the edge off Kadett were quickly dashed. He never settled well in strange places, but this was even worse than usual.

Jennie tried everything she could think of to get him to work in a relaxed fashion, but time was ticking over in the warm-up to the competition and things were rapidly going downhill. Every time she turned him to the left and asked for piaffe, Kadett would become stiff and tense, almost threatening to rear. Rocky, the team trainer, told her that he was being defiant and urged her to hit him, but Jennie knew her horse and knew that this was not the answer.

It seemed as if the British team was under a malevolent cloud. Poor Sarah Whitmore had been struck by conjunctivitis, the painful eye condition; she could barely keep her eyes open, let alone ride, so Rocky was having to lunge Junker and get him warmed up in-hand. Emotions were getting high, so Jennie decided that she needed to go and work on Kadett on her own without getting screamed at.

Rocky might have had his hands full with Sarah's horse, but he had eyes in the back of his head and was conscious of his team duties. Feeling like a naughty schoolgirl, Jennie persuaded someone to distract him at one end of the stables whilst she sneaked Kadett out of the other and went to find a working-in area out of sight. There she met Willie Schultheiss, the German team trainer who was one of the top riders of the 1950s and 1960s.

Schultheiss was renowned for being a thinking rider and Jennie, with nothing to lose, asked him for his advice. Generously, Schultheiss came over to watch her warming up Kadett and see if he could help – though she admits that one reason for his generosity might have been that the British presented absolutely no threat to the Germans! He suggested a trick that he told her often worked with horses who were stiff on one side and at his suggestion, Jennie turned Kadett in a small circle and then asked for piaffe.

It seemed to break through the barrier of resistance and although the quality of the piaffe was not particularly good, he was at least performing it. As they went into the arena Jennie knew in her heart that though Kadett was technically sound, something was not quite right and the resistance was his way of trying to tell her. She rode one of the most difficult tests of her career, persuading and cajoling the little horse to give her as much as he could without pushing him into an explosion.

Their test was reasonable, which was as much as she could have hoped for. Michael Clayton, later to become *Horse &Hound's* editor, wrote: 'Kadett was particularly disappointing as he has certainly performed better than this, but he had apparently been unsettled in training...he showed some signs of resistance in the Grand Prix, though his extensions were attractive.'

Not surprisingly, Germany won the team gold. Individual gold went to Switzerland's Christine Stuckelberger on the brilliant but unpredictable Granat, who was renowned for suddenly shooting forwards and trying to bolt. What none of the other riders or judges knew at the time was that Granat was blind in one eye and terrified by things that he could hear, but not see. His rider later said that it had been decided to keep Granat's disability secret, for fear that the judges would be prejudiced against him.

After the competition Jennie's brother, Michael, made a point of thanking the German Equestrian Federation's representative for Willie Schultheiss's helpfulness. In the course of conversation, he mentioned that Jennie and Anthony had a young horse, Dutch Courage, who showed great promise and whose future they were particularly excited about. He and Kadett had never been seen in competition together, which was a deliberate choice – now in his late teens, Kadett was showing inevitable signs of stiffness and Jennie could not bear to see him beaten by a youngster because he himself was past his best.

Difficult though he undoubtedly was, Kadett was the horse who had given Jennie her first taste of international dressage success and she felt that she owed him much more than he owed her. He spent the rest of his days at Catherston and was finally put down at the age of seventeen, when navicular – a painful condition of the feet thought to be related to arthritis – meant he no longer had quality of life. With hindsight, Jennie recognised that the start of navicular probably made advanced work uncomfortable, and that was why he showed such strong signs of resistance in Montreal.

Largely as a result of Michael's conversation, Jennie was offered a scholarship to go to Germany that winter for a short training period with Willie. He had recognised in her a talent and open mindedness that he liked and from Jennie's point of view, it was an offer she could not refuse. She was told she could take two horses and at first she planned to take Bill and a son of Xenocles called Xenarchus. Bred out of an Anglo-Arab mare, he was an advanced dressage horse who later represented Britain in the Young Riders European Championship.

Unfortunately, he cracked a bone just before Jennie was due to leave and had to be box rested, so in the end Jennie loaded Bill and a homebred youngster called Catherston Credit into the lorry and went off to Germany by herself, leaving Anthony to look after Anne and Lizzie with her secretary, Bridget White, now Thompson, and Bridget's young son, Gavin. Bridget was just one of many people who came to work at Catherston and ended up as a good friend. Jenny Care, who started there in the 1970s and soon became known as Care Bear, was another secretary who became part of the family.

By the time Jennie went to Schultheiss, she had also managed to establish Bill's passage. To try and help him understand what was wanted, Jennie took him into the river in the hope that the deep water would encourage him to offer the correct movement. Unfortunately, what worked for Kadett did not work for Bill. When training horses, Jennie has always followed the philosophy that there are no problems, only solutions, and that if one approach does not work, you try others until you find the one that does.

On her travels in America, she had seen hackneys trained to exaggerate the breed's naturally high-stepping trot with the use of lunge reins attached to their front legs. With the help of Paul Fielder, later a

top rider and trainer in his own right, she adopted a similar approach with Bill. With Jennie holding one lunge rein and Paul the other, she asked Bill to trot and they gently pulled on the appropriate reins to encourage the stallion to flex his joints. Timing was everything, and as soon as Bill got the idea – which, being such an intelligent horse, did not take him long – he was given lots of rewards. Soon passage was as much a part of his repertoire as piaffe.

Travelling alone with two horses would be daunting for any rider, but for someone as shy as Jennie it was a prospect far more frightening than entering an Olympic dressage arena. As soon as she knew she was going, she put herself through a Linguaphone 'teach yourself German' course, but although it covered basic day to day conversation, the ability to ask for directions to the nearest railway station were not terribly useful on a specialised dressage yard.

Willie – who Jennie admits she was terrified of – spoke little English, but even so it was better than her German. She came down on her first morning and asked for a cup of coffee in her best Linguaphone accent, only to be answered in English. Later she realised that the others were trying to put her at ease, but at the time it was a little dispiriting!

121

Willie suggested that on the first day, she should watch what went on and familiarise herself with the set-up whilst her horses settled in. She soon realised that efficiency was as much a byword in this top training yard as it was throughout the rest of Germany; horses were never rushed, but time was precious and every minute put to good use. As she took her seat at the side of the school, Jennie wondered why there were lots of stirrup irons and leathers hanging on the wall. As the first pupils came in, she found out – each led a horse into the school and mounted with one stirrup, which was then unhooked from the saddle and hung on the wall.

Deciding that if this was the way things were done, it was the way she had to follow, Jennie brought in Dutch Courage for her first lesson with one stirrup on her saddle. As soon as she had mounted, she took it off, hung it on the wall and rode the stallion without stirrups. Fortunately, he was interested in his new surroundings but remained calm, and Jennie's fear that she might be sent into orbit proved groundless.

After asking Jennie what she had done with Bill so far, Willie watched her warm up. He said very little, which she was not sure was good or bad, then asked if he could ride the stallion. Willie rode Bill brilliantly and the stallion – who until then had only been ridden by Jennie – was happy and confident. Together they performed canter pirouettes, zigzags and flying changes whilst Jennie watched.

Understandably, she watched with mixed feelings. On the one hand, it was wonderful to see the horse she had brought on from scratch performing so well. But on the other, she could not help wondering how Bill's performance with Willie compared to how he went for her. Willie, however, was full of praise for the way Bill's work had been established.

Over the next six weeks Jennie had only a couple of formal lessons; the training system worked more along the lines of pupils working their horses alongside the trainers, who would comment as and when they felt they needed to. Although far less structured than a formal lesson, it perhaps developed the rider's ability to think and work through problems. It also gave her a greater understanding of terms which she feels many British riders misinterpreted, with dire results for their riding and their horses.

In particular, she learned that what had been translated as 'sitting deep' did not mean, as many riders and trainers assumed, sitting heavily and driving down with the seat. Instead, it meant raising the diaphragm and allowing the horse's back to come up underneath the rider's seat – by keeping a toned, balanced posture, the rider would help and encourage the horse to stay in balance. In recent years, fashionable trainers who talk about the horse echoing the rider's posture, or who maintain that a balanced seat means that if the horse was taken away from underneath her a rider should land on her feet, have been hailed as if they were the new Messiahs. In fact, this is the way Jennie has been riding since she was a child, with posture and balance learned partly through playing cowboys and Indians on ponies and later through a mixture of training and her own realisation of what gave the results she wanted.

As Jennie's training with Willie Schultheiss progressed, the riders and trainers became more and more interested in Dutch Courage. 'The English girl' who had been looked on as just another pupil with just another horse when she arrived had shown that she and her horse had talent and ability that could not be ignored. Towards the end of her stay, the director of the German federation came to watch Jennie working Bill and commented that he was a very, very good horse.

Pleased by the compliment, Jennie was not prepared for what came next. 'And how much would you want for him?' inquired the director. With barely a split second pause, Jennie replied that Dutch Courage was not for sale at any price, though she appreciated the offer. She knew that she had probably turned down a sum that could have made any financial worries a thing of the past, but neither she nor Anthony ever regretted her instinctive reaction. Dutch Courage was a horse of a lifetime, and as such was beyond price.

Returning home, Jennie was grateful that she had been able to experience those six intensive weeks but glad to see Anthony and their daughters again. She still could not quite believe that Bill had reached top level so quickly – he was at Prix St Georges level by the time he was six – and used her friendship with a girl called Bridget Maxwell, a former student at Catherston, to make sure she was not pushing him too far, too soon. Bridget had also been to a top German trainer, Herbert

Rehbein, who had many horses of about the same age as Bill. Just as proud and occasionally anxious parents will compare notes on their offspring's progress, Jennie would say to Bridget: 'Bill's doing this, what are your horses doing?'

Dutch Courage was so talented and so quick to learn that she had to keep pinching herself. Her instincts and experience told her that training must be progressive and that it was important to keep Bill confident and happy in his work. But if Bill had been a child, he would have forever been asking 'Can I do this?' and 'Let's try this next.' He was a fast-track whizzkid who loved what he did and found most of it easy and by 1977, the dressage world was taking notice.

Jennie and he were chosen as members of the British team competing in the European Championships in St Galen, Switzerland. It was an unheard of achievement for an eight-year-old and Jennie faced a daunting prospect that demanded cool nerves and the ability to cope with pressure. At this time Christine Stuckelberger and the great, charismatic Granat were at the height of their career, but Dutch Courage – very much the new boy on the block – put up an amazing performance to finish ninth individually.

Suddenly dressage started to become more fashionable. Even the non-specialist equestrian press started to ask what it was all about and in 1978, Jennie was approached by the *Sunday Telegraph* magazine to see if they could do an interview with her. The combination of a young, attractive rider and her charismatic stallion was irresistible and a journalist and photographer came out to turn them into cover stars and publicise that year's World Championships, which were being held at Goodwood.

Behind the glamorous pictures that captivated thousands of readers enjoying their weekend breakfasts was a day fraught with incident. The *Sunday Telegraph* wanted a mix of glamour, excitement and the 'aah' factor to try and get across the message that dressage had it all. The glamour was easy enough once Jennie managed to overcome her shyness at being photographed; Bill had no such reservations and was a natural in front of the cameras. Like so many truly great horses, he had a natural presence that demanded 'Look at me!' Old horsemen sometimes call it 'the look of eagles' and Bill possessed it in abundance.

The excitement came when it was suggested that one of the photographs should show Jennie lungeing a grey stallion, Courageous – one of Bill's first sons – as part of their preparation. To her mortification, Courageous gave full rein to his sense of humour and bucked and snorted for all he was worth. It must, she recalls with amusement, have looked like something out of the Wild West.

All that was left was the 'aah' factor, and the photographer suggested that this could be provided by a shot showing Jennie with one of the foals. They made their way out to the fields and the photographer was delighted to find one lying down with its dam. Jennie did not share his pleasure, as she realised that the reason the foal had not got up on their approach was that it had injured its leg.

Thinking on her feet, she let him take a quick photograph of her holding it then immediately arranged for it to be rushed off to the vet. The foal must have been kicked by another mare for being too inquisitive, because it turned out that its leg was broken. Fortunately they had discovered it in time for the leg to be pinned and the limb healed.

When the magazine came out, on the very weekend of the championships, the article and photographs gave British dressage the best publicity it had ever had. It was a triumph – but also a terrible responsibility. As she read the glowing report about how Britain was no longer the poor relation, but had riders and horses that could take on the best in the world, Jennie felt as if she was walking a tightrope. If all went well, she could be pleased that she and Bill had done their bit to enhance the profile of dressage in this country. If it did not… quite simply, it did not bear thinking about.

Bill, who had no doubts about his own importance, did nothing for Jennie's confidence as the championships started. She was nervous and he was full of himself and the combination produced a disappointing start that, in Jennie's eyes, verged on the disastrous. Bill had so much energy he did not know what to do with it, and in the first test he went totally over the top and did not listen to her. Some of his work was brilliant, but unfortunately this was cancelled out by marks lost through inattention and tension. Jennie rode out of the arena feeling disappointed and despondent.

However, she was also determined that no one should have grounds for saying that she and Bill could not take the pressure. It was not her own reputation that she was worried about, but that of her horse and the team: she knew he could perform far better and that she had to get him into a state of mind where he would use his energy and brilliance in a positive, not negative, way. She also knew that if she simply tried to drill him she would lose the enthusiasm and sparkle that made him so special – she needed to find a way of keeping those qualities by channelling his excess energy into something he would enjoy and which would relax him without losing that vital edge.

Jennie explained all this to Ernst Bachinger, the British team coach, and told him what she had in mind. Ernst thought her suggestion was rather unorthodox, but accepted that she knew her horse and his temperament. Accordingly, Jennie and Bill headed off for the racehorse gallops at Goodwood, where anyone watching would have been astonished to see Britain's top dressage prospects working out at a rate that any racehorse trainer would have been proud of. This started to unwind the spiral of tension and Bill came out next day on his toes, but on the same wavelength as his rider.

Leaving nothing to chance, Jennie worked the stallion for two and a half hours before the Grand Prix. As soon as he entered the arena she knew that this time they were working in partnership rather than her having to try and outwit him. Bill was ready to listen to what she asked him to do rather than insisting on setting his own agenda, and as they came down the centre line for the final time Jennie knew that whilst he was a little tired, they had given a much better account of themselves.

They finished in eighth place, which was a good result by any standards, but even whilst she was accepting the congratulations of friends and supporters Jennie knew that Bill was still not working at his best. She had one more chance, as they had qualified for the Special – the individual ride-off. For this competition, riders went in drawn order, and when the draw was made Jennie could have been forgiven for thinking that the fates were stacked against her. She and Bill were first to go.

Jennie had only ridden the Special once before and was in a terrible quandary. She knew that although Bill had been co-operative in the

126

Grand Prix, he had not been at his brilliant best. To coax that from him, she had to literally ride a tightrope between settling his mind and keeping his exuberance. If she played safe and worked him hard before the test, she ran the risk of tipping the balance too far to the side of obedience; if she did too little, there was the risk that he would explode.

Bachinger could advise, but he did not know Bill as well as Jennie did and in the end, it was her decision. She decided that rather than riding him in for two hours, she would lunge him first to keep his muscles soft and stretched. She then led him around for half an hour, letting him pick at grass and soak up the atmosphere.

With an hour and a half to go, Jennie got on him and worked on the basics, making sure that he was alert and at the same time free from tension; it sounds an impossible combination, but it is only when a horse is switched on mentally and physically that he can perform at his best. For the last half an hour, Jennie worked Bill with Bachinger looking on. He was able to offer suggestions on fine tuning, but accepted that Jennie and Bill were already in harmony and that his job at this stage was to encourage and support her.

As soon as they entered the arena, Jennie knew that Bill wanted to give his best. He seemed to grow taller underneath her, as if to say 'OK, let's stop messing about and show them what we can do.'

And what they did was quite extraordinary. Bill was soft, fluid, but full of impulsion. At every stride he was listening and waiting to see what she wanted him to do next, but without trying to anticipate. When it came to the piaffe, it was like sitting on a controlled volcano – and it looked as good as it felt. One of the judges awarded them nine marks out of a possible ten for this movement, an accolade rarely given.

Jennie knew that Bill had done his best, but even when their score was announced neither she nor the people watching realised just how brilliant it had been. Hers was the first mark to be announced, and although she was delighted she fully expected that there would be several others who would achieve better. But as rider followed rider and the line of scores lengthened on the board, she stayed where she had started, at the top.

At first even Jennie found it hard to believe. The reality of what they had achieved only began to sink in when she realised that she had beaten riders she had never beaten before, such as Harry Boldt. Excitement grew amongst the spectators and the young Pony Club members whose job was to collect the judges' score sheet kept coming up to her with big grins to announce 'You've beaten another one!'

With just two riders to go, Dutch Courage was in the lead. Those two – Switzerland's Christine Stuckelberger on Granat and Uwe Schulten-Baumer with Slibowitz for Germany – took it from her. Even so, nothing could undermine the fact that Jennie and Dutch Courage, the little horse who had come off the lorry breathing fire and looking like a racehorse, had won a bronze medal for Britain at the World Championships, in front of a home crowd.

Later that year, Jennie went out to Austria for a training clinic with Ernst Bachinger. Thanks to the generosity of dressage enthusiast Kay Hinckley, she and other riders – Stephen Clarke, Diana Mason and Bar Hammond – were able to take their horses to him in Vienna. The Hinckley family, who had a large estate near Doncaster, started dressage competitions there and also sponsored Bachinger to come to Britain.

Jennie remembers that training trip as much for her new-found skills as a farrier as for the riding. Although the Continentals were the masters of training, their skills in handling and looking after horses sometimes fell short of the ideal. Bar's horse needing shoeing, but objected to what was the standard practice there of one person holding up the horse's leg whilst another banged on the shoe. The farriers could not even get the old shoes off, let alone put the new ones on.

Whenever anyone had a problem with their horse, it was always 'Let's see what Jennie can do' – something that has not changed. The horse was very nervous, but became calmer when handled by a woman. Jennie managed to remove the shoes, trim its feet and put on a new set. Her biggest fear was not that she would get kicked, but whether or not she could manage to nail on the shoes without driving a nail outside the 'safe' area of the hoof within which the horse feels no pain. Fortunately, it came out sound the next morning and remained so.

One day offered a rare chance of free time, so the riders decided to spend the day in Vienna, where they revelled in the chance to simply walk around and take in the sights. Standing in the middle of one of the main squares, they were debating where to go for lunch when one of the reception staff from their hotel came rushing up to them. Relieved that she had found them, she told them that there had been an urgent message for Jennie to contact the British Embassy.

Her first thought was that something terrible must have happened at home. Convinced that someone had died, they tried to keep calm as she found the nearest phone and rang the contact number she had been given. It was as if Jennie had stepped into a starring role in a James Bond film: the cool voice at the end of the phone would not tell her anything until she had answered a series of questions to identify herself – answers that only she could have known.

As soon as she had talked her way through the verbal maze, Jennie was reassured that she had nothing to worry about. However, she did have plenty to think about, because she was asked if she would accept the MBE in the next Honours List. Totally taken aback, and not even sure what she was accepting or why, Jennie said that she would.

She was warned that she was not allowed to tell anyone about the award, as all were kept secret until the actual publication of the list. Looking back, Jennie says that it could have been worse: when Jane was made a Lieutenant of the Royal Victorian Order, the first she or anyone else in the family knew about it was when Anthony saw it listed in a newspaper along with others in the New Year Honours. This award was a personal one from members of the Royal Family, and Jane had been a lady-in-waiting to the Princess Royal.

Being made a Member of the Order of the British Empire was recognition of Jennie's services to the equestrian world. Although she was only thirty-five at the time, she had probably done more than any other rider to raise the profile of British dressage and was one of the first breeders to appreciate the importance of a planned breeding policy. She felt that in many ways, being honoured in this way was also a tribute to her parents and the way she and the other Bullen children had been brought up to respect horses at the same time as gaining their respect.

The award ceremony was both an honour and an ordeal – far more stress-inducing than riding in competition. The local dressmaker made her a dress for the occasion and protocol dictated she also had to wear a hat. Anthony and the girls accompanied her to Buckingham Palace and Jennie, along with other recipients of that year's honours, was shown to a waiting room. Here they were given a crash course in the appropriate etiquette.

When her name was called out, Jennie was told, she should walk towards the Queen and halt in front of her. She should then curstey and respond briefly to any questions; however, she should not speak unless spoken to. When she was presented with the award, she should curtsey once again, then leave the room without turning her back on the monarch – all far more terrifying than halting on the centre line and saluting the judge.

Most of the occasion passed in a blur. However, Jennie remembers that both the Queen and the Duke of Edinburgh were pleasant and relaxed and obviously enthusiastic about her achievements. She was wearing her Duke of Edinburgh gold award and the Duke spotted this straight away, asking her what she had done and how she had enjoyed it.

Once the ceremony was over and Jennie could relax and appreciate the significance of what she had just been through, she realised that Anne, who had been as excited as any of them at the idea of going to Buckingham Palace, seemed rather quiet. It turned out that she had expected that Jennie would kneel in front of the Queen and then be tapped on the shoulder with a ceremonial sword. The reality, though quite enough of an ordeal for Jennie, did not have enough pomp and circumstance to satisfy Anne!

There was even more glory to come for the Bullen sisters that year, as both Sarah and Jane appeared in the film *International Velvet*. By now, Sarah had made her name as a successful actress, a career choice she says happened almost by default rather than choice. At the age of twenty-one she was encouraged by her family to go and study opera in Italy, both to make the most of her natural gift as a singer and to take her mind off a romance that had ended unhappily. When she returned, intending to concentrate on a singing career, she was encouraged by others in the entertainment industry to combine it with acting.

To get her Equity card, Sarah had to sing in what she cheerfully describes as some extraordinary places. Singing the blues in London nightclubs, she eventually sang her way into the possession of a coveted Equity card and began chasing roles. She still remembers her first televised role, in 1975, and it still makes her laugh almost as much as it did then. Sarah won a part in *Space 1999*, which became a cult series centred on the fortunes of the crew of the Moonbase Alpha. Every week, the crew – thrown into deep space after a massive explosion on the moon - struggled for survival.

In the first episode, Sarah, as the cool-headed Kate, was knocked off her feet in an encounter with a rogue planet. When the commander demanded 'Are you all right, Kate?' she had to tell him: 'Yes, Commander, but my equipment has taken a beating.' The cast and camera crew found it so hard not to laugh that the scene had to be reshot umpteen times.

Fortunately, her other roles were more rewarding. In the television series *The House of Caradus*, set in a mythical auction house, she played the tough Helena Caradus; she also appeared in the series of *The Perfect Spy*, based on John le Carre's novel. Her film credits include the 1987 production of Frederick Forsyth's *The Fourth Protocol*, and in the same year she made a television guest appearance as Mrs Vasilakis in 'Greeks Bearing Gifts', an episode of *Inspector Morse*.

However, it is the film *International Velvet* which she thinks of with the greatest affection, at least partly because it turned into, in her own words, 'a Bullen benefit'. Directed by Bryan Forbes, it starred the then fifteen-year-old Tatum O'Neal as the spoilt brat who ends up winning an Olympic eventing medal and, of course, becoming a truly wonderful person in the process. Sarah plays Beth, who breaks down in tears when she learns at the end of the selection process that she has not won a place on the team and wins the sympathy of everyone who has ever competed, at whatever level, whilst Jane doubled for Tatum in the difficult riding scenes. As Jennie and Jane provided horses for the film, Sarah's description of it is perhaps not such an exaggeration!

Sarah put her acting career on hold when she married businessman Peter Vey in 1986, though she says that she may be tempted into becoming a 'character actress' in years to come. For the moment, she is content to concentrate on her family – she and Peter have three sons, Charlie, born in 1988 and twins Edward and Archie who are two years younger – and her horses and ponies. Bubbly's legacy lives on in her mares – including one descended from her beloved Catherston Moon Fairy, on whom she had many showing successes – as she concentrates on breeding the larger ponies and small horses which are becoming so much in demand for today's market.

10

Alternative Glory

In 1979 Jennie was sent one of Dutch Courage's first offspring to break. Sent by his breeder, Doreen Goodall, the colt was called Dutch Gold and was the last foal from a mare called Gold K. She had produced some good youngsters, including the show hack, Tenterk, originally produced at Catherston. Tenterk, an elegant bay, was the double of Catherston Credit, and the two were shown as a pair, with Jane riding Credit and Sarah on the gelding.

On one occasion the judge was totally confused as to which horse was which. He first put up Sarah to head the line, but Tenterk, then only a five-year-old, did not give a very good individual show and changed places with Catherston Credit, who had been slotted into second place. Jane thought it was enormously funny to take the champion hack title on something that had only been shown to make up a pair, but Tenterk made up for his lapse in later years. He was champion three times running at the Horse of the Year Show and Robert Oliver, who took over the ride, described him as the perfect pattern of a hack and one of the best horses he had ever ridden.

However, Dutch Gold proved that perhaps Gold K had been saving the best until last. Jennie soon realised that he had inherited his sire's athleticism, movement and intelligence and knew that she would love to ride and compete father and son. His owner intimated that he could be for sale and although Jennie was not in a position to buy him outright, she knew someone who might be.

Businessman Donald Bannocks was already a good friend at Catherston and for a long time owned Tigre, the show jumper ridden by the brilliant Caroline Bradley. Sadly, their relationship as owner/rider hit insoluble problems and Caroline – whose riding Jennie admired enormously – lost the ride. Not long afterwards she died from a heart attack, whilst only in her thirties.

Mr Bannocks' son, Darren, had been a keen show jumper but had a bad fall from his pony. Mr Bannocks wanted to interest him in dressage instead and came to Jennie in the hope that she could help Darren to become equally successful in a different discipline. The answer came in the shape of a lovely dun mare called Blagdon Fiesta, who had been bred by Thalia Gordon-Watson, by Bubbly out of Fortune II who was also the dam of Prosperity of Catherston. Anne was riding a 14.2hh mare of similar colour called Sunday Collection, who was out of Prosperity of Catherston and the two were very successful in pairs classes.

Darren was a quiet, competent rider and Fiesta gave him just the boost he needed. Mr Bannocks used to bring him to Catherston and had a few lessons with Jennie himself so that he and Darren could hack round the New Forest with the Loriston-Clarkes. Although his enthusiasm had always been for show jumping, he became equally interested in the challenge of dressage as he watched Jennie and saw Darren progress to higher levels, first with the Prix St Georges schoolmaster Benjamin Bunny and later with the stallion, Tapster.

One morning, totally out of the blue, he rang up and told Jennie he would like to buy her a dressage horse. His timing was perfect and Jennie immediately told him about Dutch Gold; Mr Bannocks was enthusiastic about the idea of owning a son of Dutch Courage, who he much admired, and the price his owner had quoted seemed a reasonable one to him.

Jennie invited both buyer and seller into her home, introduced them and waited for the formalities of the sale to be completed. To her horror and embarrassment, it was announced that the original asking price no longer applied. It was the equivalent of gazumping and Jennie was so angry, she had to leave the room before she blew up.

Mr Bannocks, who had not built up his considerable business interests without honing equally considerable negotiating skills, was not at all phased. The wheeling and dealing continued and soon Dutch Gold had a new owner and new career prospects.

It was obvious that Willow, as he was known at home, had breeding as well as competition potential, and one of Jennie's first acts was to get him graded with the new British Warmblood Society. At that time there was still a lot of suspicion amongst British breeders over any forms of grading or registration, which some of them regarded as a waste of time and money, signs of a 'Big Brother' or both. However, Jennie was convinced right from the start that if Britain was to produce horses that could compete on equal terms with the Continentals, it was vital that we establish a proper breeding programme.

Many breeders were too complacent and short sighted. We had the Thoroughbred, the most influential horse in the world, and no one questioned the need for recording, studying and carefully selecting bloodlines in the racing world. However, when it came to other disciplines and sports, there was a feeling that if the horse was by a Thoroughbred and was half decent at its job, its ancestry did not matter.

The argument was often raised that whilst it was useful to know something about a mare's background, a gelding was only as good as the way he performed. The general argument ran that as a gelding could not be used for breeding, his parentage was irrelevant.

It was only through the work and investment of time and money by studs such as Catherston that Britain eventually began to realise that by establishing proven performance lines, we were producing better horses for any job. It was not just a case of producing dressage horses, or show jumpers, or eventers: over the past fifty years Catherston has produced equine athletes. They have chosen to route their stallions mainly to dressage careers, but the jumping ability is there and has been proven, both in the show jumping arena and the eventing circuit.

Willow is finer in build than his sire, as he has another line of Thoroughbred in his breeding. Dutch Courage could be flighty and definitely had a sense of humour, but Jennie soon found that Willow was much more like a Thoroughbred to ride. Right from the very beginning, he was a challenge: not because he was naughty, but because although he was very sensitive, she had to be positive with him.

He has always liked to work, but is sensitive to noise – both outside distractions and his rider's voice – and to touch. It was fortunate for him that he stayed with Jennie, who soon learned to understand him and enjoyed building a partnership with him. Willow began 'proper' work as a four-year-old and was rather ebullient, though his paces were so good Jennie realised that he, like his sire, was going to find a lot of his work relatively easy and would need to be kept occupied. She decided to take him to Wellington Dressage for his first outing, but things did not quite go to plan. Willow was fine in one direction, but when she asked him to turn and work on the other rein he resisted to the point of almost being nappy.

Jennie knew that there was no point in having a fight and simply kidded him around the arena. Convinced that Willow was not a nappy horse, she knew that there must be something physically wrong and that his behaviour was his way of telling her that he was uncomfortable. It turned out that the outside edges of his cheek teeth had become very sharp and were chafing the tender skin, aggravated by the slightest pressure on the reins. Once the sharp edges were rasped smooth, the discomfort disappeared and Willow was much happier.

Jennie felt that he needed something to do, so introduced him to trotting poles – poles spaced at distances compatible to the horse's stride length which encourage him to flex his joints, pick up his feet and think

Dales Pony

about where he is going. None of his older brothers and sisters could jump and Tenterk had even said 'No thank you' out hunting, which usually encourages even the most timid or reluctant jumper to leave the ground. She was therefore not at all surprised when Willow could not or would not pick up his feet over poles and was quite happy to kick them out of place.

A few weeks later Jennie took her children and Darren out for a hack in the New Forest. Hacking out has always been part of her horses' education and lifestyle, which surprises some stallion owners; however, Jennie points out that if a horse does not have the temperament to behave itself in company and can only be ridden in an arena, it probably does not have the temperament to be considered as a breeding prospect.

On this occasion, Anne was riding Double Bubble and Darren was on Fiesta. They came to a narrow, very shallow part of the river and for some reason, Fiesta decided she did not want want to go through. Anne offered to give Darren a lead, but she even refused to follow Double Bubble. Willow then decided that if Fiesta did not want to risk it, he certainly was not going to get his feet wet.

Without getting cross with him, Jennie indicated firmly that she was not prepared for him to behave like a total wimp and eventually Willow was persuaded to paddle through. Once he was in the water, he decided that this was not so bad, after all. Fiesta soon realised that she was going to be left behind and that she would rather not be, and soon all three were splashing about.

Anne and Darren wanted to jump their ponies in and out of the water, and the now much braver Willow happily joined in. Continuing on their ride, they came across a few small logs across the forest paths which were too tempting to ride round. The ponies flew over them and, much to Jennie's surprise, so did Willow. The horse who could not pick up his feet over trotting poles had suddenly decided that the real thing was much more fun. Jennie remembers that when they got back, she remarked to Mr Bannocks that she thought Dutch Gold might actually go eventing.

Later that year, she decided to take him to a novice event near Brighton, where she knew the fences would be well designed. Willow did a lovely dressage test and popped round the show jumping course in a style that showed he had completely forgotten his earlier contempt of coloured poles. So far his only experience of cross-country had been going in the river and jumping logs in the forest, so Jennie was not sure what to expect of him in the final phase.

Knowing that the only thing to do was think positive, she cantered him towards the first inviting fence on the cross-country course. Willow, who was not quite sure what he was supposed to do, weaved towards it and jumped in careful, exaggerated fashion. He treated the second fence in the same cautious manner then, at fence three, suddenly decided that he knew what he was doing and was actually enjoying himself.

His ears were pricked and his canter rhythmic and confident as he tackled the rest of the course. To Jennie's delight, the stallion that no one had thought would leave the ground came seventh in his first event.

As Dutch Gold was making his first forays into competition, his sire was heading towards the peak of his career. Dutch Courage was then eleven years old and arguably the most talented British produced dressage horse yet. In 1980, an Olympic year, he gave his supporters real hope that he and Jennie might be the first ever British pair to win an Olympic medal, hope that was reinforced when he made a triumphant appearance at Goodwood.

By this time Bill was physically and mentally mature. His paces had developed and he had even more charisma; Jennie had also benefited from training with Ernst Bachinger. Bill came out ready and able to take on the world. His Grand Prix test was superb and he won not only that, but the FEI Grand Prix Special and Intermediaire II competitions. It was an incredible hat trick and amongst the riders Jennie beat was the leading German professional, Georg Theodorescu. Hearing the national anthem played to celebrate her victory was a special moment for Jennie, made even more special by the fact that it was on home ground.

The dressage world was rapidly becoming more international and love of their sport and for their horses broke down the barriers between riders. Unfortunately, that was not reflected in the world outside and later that year, Russia invaded Afghanistan. Political protest was immediate and sportsmen and women throughout the world boycotted the Moscow Olympics – though not always by choice.

The horse world's governing bodies responded quickly to the Soviet Union's outrageous act. Giving up the chance to compete in an Olympics, the ultimate in any sporting career, is a momentous decision, but the British Equestrian Federation had no hesitation in making it.

Athletes in all disciplines, including the riders, had differing views on whether or not the decision of the BEF and athletics' organising bodies was the right one. Although horror at what was happening in Afghanistan was universal, not everyone agreed with the boycott. Some competitors believed that sport was being made a tool of politicians and that boycotting the Games actually devalued the Olympic spirit.

Jennie felt and still does feel that although the situation in Afghanistan was abhorrent, not going to the Olympic Games made no difference to the outcome of the war. She believes that politics and sport have, or should have, nothing to do with each other and that sportsmen and women should not be used as pawns. However, these views made no difference at the time: the decision was made at government level.

To try and give competitors something to mark the training and preparation they had put in, competitions were organised at different venues. Soon dubbed the 'Alternative Olympics', they could not match the real thing for atmosphere and occasion, but at least they provided competition and a way of demonstrating the strength of feeling throughout the sporting world.

Goodwood, the home of British dressage, was chosen as the venue for the Alternative Olympics dressage. Apart, obviously, from the Russians, only one top international rider went to Moscow – Austria's Sissy Theurer. She won the individual gold medal, but in the eyes of the world it was tarnished and of little if any value. The real competition, officially called a festival, was at Goodwood. Inchcape PLC provided the main sponsorship and the government, eager to show its recognition of the BEF's stand, also provided funds so that another international arena could be put down. The Prime Mininster, Margaret Thatcher, made her first and probably last appearance at a dressage competition to thank the riders for boycotting the Moscow Olympics.

Goodwood was always one of Bill's favourite venues. He had definite likes and dislikes and never liked the setting for the Horse of the Year

Show dressage competitions. These were held at a riding stables near Harrow, in what to Jennie was a perfectly acceptable indoor school. The only reason she can think of for Bill's dislike of it was that it did not have enough atmosphere to satisfy his extrovert personality, and he never went his best there.

No one could say that the 'Alternative Olympics' competition at Goodwood was second rate, though this was certainly true of the dressage in Moscow. All the great riders came to Britain: Christine Stuckelberger with Granat and Turmalin, the late Reiner Klimke with Ahlerich and Uwe Schulten-Baumer and Slibowitz. Germany took the team gold, Switzerland silver and Denmark bronze, with Britain sixth.

Christine Stuckelberger and Granat seemed invincible and no one was surprised when they also won individual gold. Uwe Schulten-Baumer and Reiner Klimke took silver and bronze respectively for Germany – and to the delight of his rider and her country, Dutch Courage finished in sixth place. It was a test full of power and expression and at eleven years of age, Dutch Courage surely still had one more chance to win real Olympic Glory.

11

'The Whole World in His Hands'

The early eighties saw Jennie riding on a high. Dutch Courage was in his prime and Jennie was looking ahead to the 1984 Olympics, to be held in Los Angeles. She knew that with horses, nothing is ever certain, but their partnership was becoming even stronger and the selectors looked on them as one of Britain's strongest hopes.

Much to Jennie's delight, Anne and Lizzie were both showing both a confirmed love of horses and natural talent, though in very individual ways. Anne was the outwardly bold, confident one of the two and was able to throw off what must have been the pressure as well as the pleasure of being Jennie Loriston-Clarke's daughter; right from the start, she knew what she wanted to do – and what did not appeal. She even managed to get herself 'expelled' from ballet lessons by informing her teacher that she really could not turn her toes out because it would be bad for her riding position!

As she started to make her mark in dressage, she had more than her fair share of people saying 'Oh well, you're bound to be good, look whose daughter you are' – something Lizzie was also to hear, so many times. But although they recognised and appreciated the opportunities they had in terms of horses and encouragement, they were also taught that success is something that has to be worked for. They were always encouraged to follow their own interests; Lizzie found quite soon that

141

dressage was her main love, but Anne loved jumping: as a little girl, she was always wanting to see how high she could jump. Later on, this boldness was channelled into eventing.

Anne was also an accomplished driver; the Welsh Cob stallion, Bryn-y-Mor Comet, was one of her favourites at Catherston and she had a lot of success with him both under saddle and in harness. His owners, John and Mary Holmes, encouraged her driving ambitions, which were boosted enormously as a teenager by winning a scholarship from the magazine *Harpers and Queen*. This enabled her to train with Frank and Cynthia Haydon, whose names are as legendary in the driving world as Jennie's is in dressage. Anne learned an enormous amount from them and although it played no part in her enthusiasm for the sport, the fact that neither her mother nor her aunts had driven other than for fun allowed her the satisfaction of forging her own path.

Lizzie's first serious dressage partner was Lucan, a 14.2hh pony sent to Catherston for schooling by his exasperated owners, who could not catch him. Jennie's answer was to tether him out in the field, where he soon learned that it was impossible to get away and gave in with good grace. Gradually Lucan became easier to catch, but when his owners came to visit him he reverted to his old behaviour. They decided to have him put down, but he was such a nice pony and moved so well that Jennie could not see this happen and offered to buy him.

Lucan, who was supposed to be half Welsh and half Hackney – a high-stepping carriage breed – repaid her many times over for giving him a chance. Lizzie and he proved that size does not necessarily matter and on several occasions, beat much bigger horses. Jennie was particularly proud when Lizzie and Lucan finished second in the national Medium championships, which were won that year by Alan Doxey. He headed the line-up on a 17hh horse, and next to him stood Lizzie on a 14.2hh pony.

One of their greatest achievements was coming eighth in the Pony European Championships, though they nearly did not make it into the arena, let alone the prizegiving line-up. The competition was held at Saumur, in France, and Lizzie and the pony had gone on ahead with Paul Fielder, who was also training her. All competitors had to show their animals' passports to prove that vaccinations were in order, but the vet had not returned Lucan's and the organisers would not accept a faxed copy. Anthony Bullen came to the rescue with his small private plane and offered to fly out with Jennie and the passport.

Heading into Saumur airport was a hair-raising experience. Anthony announced that they would have to go in low so that Jennie could read the signposts, but it was not until the last minute that Jennie realised just how low he meant. They landed safely, only to hit their next problem: it was a Sunday morning and the airport was deserted, with not even a taxi in sight.

The resourceful Jennie and Anthony managed to thumb a lift in a butcher's van and when they explained that they were trying to find a horse competition, the obliging driver seemed to know where it was being held. Unfortunately, they found themselves arriving not at a dressage arena but at a cross-country competition. Realising that they were getting seriously worried, their good Samaritan cheerfully offered to try again.

This time, they ended up at the right venue, but with only ten minutes to go before Lucan was due in the arena. He and Lizzie went in and performed a good test, Jennie showed the pony's passport to the officials and everyone was happy – especially Jennie, who as she prepared to fly home with Anthony knew that this time, he would not have to hedge hop so that she could read the signposts.

As a little girl, Lizzie was tiny, but as a teenager, made up for lost time and grew very tall, very quickly. By the time she was fifteen her long legs meant that she needed to be riding horses rather than ponies, and for her fifteenth birthday, Jennie gave her the chestnut mare Catherston Dauntless. She thought that teaming a redhead with a redhead might be something of a gamble, but it was an incredibly successful partnership and Lizzie took the mare to Advanced level.

In 1983 Jennie and Dutch Courage had a busy international season and their timetable meant they had to compete in Denmark and from there, drive on to Aachen. Whenever Anthony's work commitments permitted, competing became a family affair: he was particularly good at navigating and would take care of this and the cooking en route whilst Jennie drove, taking over at the wheel whenever she needed a break. However, on this occasion he had to stay at home, though Jennie was able to take Anne with her.

The journey to Denmark was uneventful and Bill went so well in the Grand Prix that he qualified for the Special, a competition only open to those who had achieved the highest places in the previous classes. Jennie left the stallion in the stables for a short while whilst she went to take care of a minor administrative problem and when she returned, was informed by Anne that two members of the Russian team had showed her how to pick the lock on the door! Jennie, understandably horrified, took Bill out and was even more horrified when she took off his bandages and found that he had swelling in one of his front legs.

He looked sound when she had him trotted up in hand, so she tacked him up and began to warm up for the individual competition. Bill was happy to work and felt sound, so Jennie began to relax and think that the swelling was simply the result of standing still for a while. She made her way to the working-in arena, which necessitated riding down a track with deep going and hidden stones, and when she put him into trot felt that he was very slightly unlevel.

Neither the chef d'equipe nor the other British team members noticed that anything was wrong as she warmed up and with minutes to go, Jennie had to decide what to do. As it was an individual competition, she could have pulled out without affecting anyone else, but she felt that she was still riding for Britain and had a responsibility towards her country. If she had been at all worried about Bill, Jennie would have withdrawn him, but the problem was so minor she was the only one to realise it was there and thought he might have trodden on a stone on the way down.

Confident that she was not doing him any harm, Jennie rode through the test. Bill was willing, but his trot stride was not quite as powerful as usual and the judges' marks reflected this. She came out of the arena knowing that however minor the problem was, she could not ask Bill to perform at Aachen.

Unfortunately, other team horses were being carried on her lorry, so she had to go on to Aachen rather than going straight home even though she had decided Bill could not compete. More trouble was ahead, for driving down the autobahn, there was an enormous bang – the inside tyre had blown. Jennie managed to cruise into a parking space and then had to face the next problem on this ill-fated journey. How on earth was she going to change the wheel, which was a demanding task even for a strong man? Even more worrying, the temperature was soaring and in those days, horseboxes did not have the air conditioning which these days makes international transport so much less stressful.

What they needed was a knight in shining armour. He came to their rescue in the unlikely guise of a very large German lorry driver with an impressive beer gut, whose efforts in removing the wheel nuts were so great that Jennie was worried that he was going to have a heart attack. Finally, with sweat pouring off him, he replaced the wrecked tyre with the spare and waved Jennie off on her journey after refusing to take any payment for his work. When she reached Aachen, she had to sit and watch everyone else ride and try and find a vet to check out Dutch Courage. It turned out that the problem was a very slight ligament strain, which recovered after six weeks' rest, but she was never completely sure whether the incident with the Russians was coincidence, or if Bill had been 'got at'.

That same year, Jennie had her first proper meeting with a human dynamo called Desi Dillingham, who was to become not only one of her greatest friends and an important part of the Catherston team but a major force in British dressage. In some ways, Jennie and Desi could not be more different: Jennie is shy and hates being part of a crowd, whilst Desi is the life and soul of any party. But despite that, they have much in common – a knack of finding the solution to any problem no matter how many ways they have to approach it, a passion for horses and dressage and, when necessary, single-minded determination.

Their paths had crossed briefly in 1976, when Jennie was competing Kadett, but it was to be another seven years before they really got to know each other. Desi, a Canadian who had been a top junior show jumper and also evented successfully, had just started Masterlock Recruitment, specialising in the top sector of the employment world. It was the ideal environment for someone with her incredible energy, but although she was first and foremost a successful businesswoman she had retained her love of horses and wanted a personal involvement in the equestrian world. For Desi, it would not have been enough to simply see her company's name as a competition sponsor, though this did happen; she wanted her involvement with horses to become much more hands-on.

Jennie's enthusiasm for her horses and for dressage struck an answering chord, and Desi – already a great fan of Dutch Courage – came to Catherston to meet Bill, Dutch Gold and other talented young-sters who were waiting in the wings. Amongst them was a big chestnut named Dutch Bid and White Christmas, who Anne was to compete in Young Riders classes. Two years later, after the Los Angeles Olympics had been and gone, Desi began sponsoring these three.

Los Angeles should have been the pinnacle of Dutch Courage's career. Jennie looks on it as the biggest 'if only' in her competitive life, the chance that disappeared only days before she and Bill were due to make what should have been their last Olympic appearance. Yet she looks on it not so much as her loss, but in terms of her beloved horse never having the chance to prove himself as he should have done.

Just days before they were due to fly out, Jennie started to feel that Bill was not quite right. He looked the picture of health, but she knew him so well that she was sure that he was slightly stiff and not moving quite as freely as he should. Technically, he looked sound and it was only the close relationship she had built up with the stallion that enabled her to trust her instincts and accept that she was not imagining things in the pressurised build-up to the Olympics.

Hacking him out on the forest convinced her that there was a problem, however slight. Bill was perfectly obedient, but lacked his normal presence and sparkle, so Jennie called in her vet. His first impres-sion was that she was worrying about nothing, because when he saw Bill on the lunge everything seemed fine to his eye. However, appreci-ating that Jennie knew the horse better than anyone, he asked her to lunge him in the opposite direction – and this time, agreed that perhaps there was a slight problem, as Bill was marginally lame. The degree was so slight that it was barely perceptible, and if Jennie had not alerted him to her worries even the vet, with his trained eye, would probably not have noticed.

John McEwan, the vet to the British Olympic teams, was called in immediately. Again, his first impression was that Jennie was imagining things, but a closer examination proved otherwise. When he picked up Bill's front legs, the stallion was unable to flex his fetlock and knee joints – and the effort obviously caused him a lot of pain, because he reared in protest.

Cautiously, McEwan flexed Bill's knee again and asked Jennie to trot him up. As he moved away, the stallion was crippled. With time ticking away, it was a devastating situation – particularly for Jennie, who had trained Bill to the peak of perfection, but also for the British team as a whole. Bill was its brightest hope, the foundation of what everyone hoped could be a strong team performance, and now that foundation was crumbling.

Although there was obviously a problem, it only showed in such dramatic form when Bill's joints were manipulated to cause maximum stress. When he was ridden, there was so little sign that anything was wrong that only Jennie was really aware of it. Because of this, and because there was no obvious cause such as heat or swelling in his limbs, it was suggested that one option might be to go ahead with the flight to Los Angeles and to compete Bill on phenylbutazone, a universally used anti-inflammatory drug.

Nowadays, the use of bute is banned in competition, but in 1984, it could have been used without contravening competition rules. However, Jennie's reaction was immediate and definite: if Bill had a problem, there was no way she was going to put him under the stress of travelling and competing, no matter what honours were at stake. She had never competed a horse on bute and was adamant that she was not going to make an exception, for whilst the anti-inflammatory powders might mask the pain enough for Bill to perform, she had no way of knowing what the long-term consequences would be.

The carefully laid plans of the British team were thrown into uproar. Diana Mason, who at one stage had been aiming for a place with her horse, Prince Consort, was going to Los Angeles as chef d'equipe and as a result, had turned Prince Consort out for a holiday. Immediately and with enormous generosity, she offered to bring him up again so that Jennie could ride him instead of Dutch Courage.

The other option was that Jennie should be left out of the team and her place given to Tanya Larrigan and Salute, who had also been on the Olympic squad for Moscow. Tanya is an incredible horsewoman who was born into the circus world and has probably broken down more barriers between the different disciplines in the horse world than anyone else. An expert in classical dressage, long reining, driving, Western riding and liberty work, she is now as equally well-known for her long-reining displays with her team of miniature Shetlands. Salute was Swedish bred and came to Tanya with plenty of quirks: in her book *New Sensations for Horse and Rider* (J A Allen 2000) she says that fortunately for her, he was the horse that no one else wanted. However, they formed a wonderful partnership and Salute brought Tanya into the big time dressage world.

Solitaire & Mystic Ray

The selectors found it impossible to make up their minds. Tanya and Salute had proved that they had the ability, but Tanya lacked Jennie's international experience. Prince Consort's holiday ended abruptly as he was brought in and shod and Jennie was asked to go and ride him at Towerlands equestrian centre in Essex in front of the selectors. Getting the best out of a horse you have never sat on is the ultimate challenge, but Jennie tried to adapt her style and technique to the way Diana explained that she rode the horse, with good results.

Jennie did not really think that she would make the team on an unknown horse, but the selectors decided that there should be a competition between her and Tanya to see which partnership achieved the highest marks in a test situation. They rode the Grand Prix test and on that day, Prince Consort's mark was the higher. It was decided that Jennie would stay on the team.

Sadly for Britain's medal hopes, that first test was the best Prince Consort produced. A few days later, when they rode into the Olympic arena, he had gone slightly over the top, with the result that he became tense and so sensitive that Jennie could not ask as much as she wanted from him for fear that he would explode. She felt that by then, he had become fed up with working in an arena and would have benefited from a good gallop to relax him mentally and physically, but did not want to interfere with the training regime of someone else's horse.

She assesses their Olympic performance as fair, but with too many mistakes to leave them anywhere in contention, and they finished in thirtieth place individually. Her fellow team members, brother and sister Christopher and Jane Bartle, rode superbly and Christopher finished sixth individually on the former racehorse, Wily Trout – the highest place ever achieved by a British rider in an Olympic dressage competition. Jane and Pinocchio were twelfth individually and the team finished in eighth place. Jennie believes that if bad luck had not robbed Dutch Courage of his place, the team should have won the bronze medal. It is this 'if only' scenario that she finds so sad about Dutch Courage's career; as she puts it, he never had the chance to make his name in the way she would have liked.

The other losers in this no-win situation were, of course, Tanya and

Salute. Both she and Jennie were in impossible positions, but Jennie says that Tanya behaved with friendliness and dignity from start to finish. It was a situation that caused enormous controversy in the horse world as a whole, not just amongst dressage enthusiasts. The letters column of *Horse & Hound*, so often the forum for discussion and argument, was filled with opposing views — all so much easier to arrive at with the benefit of hindsight! Nevertheless, there was a strong feeling that Salute should have been given his chance at Olympic glory.

The final verdict on poor Dutch Courage, after blood tests were carried out at the Animal Health Trust in Newmarket, was that he had been struck by a flu-type virus not known in the UK which he must have picked up when competing in Aachen the month before. Ironically, rumours had abounded in the run-up to the Olympics that a series of viruses were sweeping through Kentucky and at one time, questions were being asked about whether the British horses should travel.

It took a good three months before Bill was anything like his old self and Jennie was able to bring him back into work. He resumed his competition career and had several good wins over the next few months, but she felt that he was not as supple through his back as he had been before the virus. In 1985, Jennie decided to retire him at the age of sixteen. He had given her his best and she wanted to repay that by retiring him from competition before he started to get beaten by horses who in other circumstances would not have been able to match his ability and expression.

Jennie wanted to make Bill's retirement from competition into a special occasion. He had always liked and gone brilliantly at Goodwood, and she was thrilled when she was allowed to hold his farewell party there. She rode him for the last time in public in the arena where he had achieved so much, and the tears in her eyes were matched by those watching as they made a final round in passage and piaffe to what had become his theme tune, *He's Got the Whole World in His Hands*.

Bill had already founded a dynasty and was joined by some of his progeny. Amongst them was Dutch Gold, who that year was starting to compete at Grand Prix level, and Catherston Dutch Bid, who went on to win a record number of Prix St Georges competitions. The youngest member of the party was a yearling son called Catherston Dazzler, who was to become yet another superstar. Bill was not only enormously talented himself, he produced enormously talented offspring.

Trying to compare horses of different generations is always difficult, but Jennie believes that Bill would have rated favourably alongside stars such as Anky van Grunsven's Olympic Bonfire. She says that Bill's strengths were in his piaffe and passage. Being critical, in a way that perhaps she alone has the right to be, Jennie says that the quality of his trot was the weakest link in that he did not show quite enough spring and elasticity. Then again, she believes that perhaps she did not ask for quite enough to bring out those qualities to the maximum.

Dutch Bid, known at home as Cassidy, was what Jennie describes as 'a real pain' as a youngster; he was bored growing up and doing nothing and it was not until he was four and being ridden that he seemed happy with his lot. In many ways he had stallion potential, but although he was a kind, much-loved horse, Jennie did not feel that he had the right temperament to stay entire and he was gelded. He was, though, an incredibly talented horse: in one year, he won the Novice, Elementary and Medium British dressage championships. His talent was wide ranging and versatile – as a six-year-old, he won the working hunter championship at the prestigious Royal Show. He also won both the novice and open finals of what was then called the Spillers dressage with jumping, where competitors had to perform a dressage test and jump a sizeable course.

At first, Cassidy seemed to have it all and soon made his mark as a team horse with Anne in Young Riders. In 1986, a year after Desi's sponsorship began, the Young Riders British team went to the European Championships in Kronenburg, Germany. Jennie had sold White Christmas to buy a bigger lorry and this was its first outing, but the trip did not have an auspicious start: the weather was atrocious and they were held up at Dover Docks for so long that they arrived at the last minute. Dutch Bid, who was always prone to travel sickness, arrived with a high temperature and their first task was to rush round to find a vet who could treat him.

Fortunately he made a rapid recovery, but because they had arrived so late, the riders were allowed to take the last three places in the competition. Although the other competitors and trainers were sympathetic, no one really felt it would make much difference to their chances: Britain was very much the longshot team. At that time dressage had the image of being a sport for older riders and did not attract younger riders the way it does today. The other nations had teams of five, but Britain could only field four riders: Anne and Dutch Bid, Nicky Sparrow (now Nicky Barrett) and Slightly Trendy, Fiona Rutland and Troy and Sara Mills and Van Dyke. To put the strengths of the competition in perspective, the German team included a slim blonde called Nicole Uphoff riding Rembrandt; two years later, they went to the Seoul Olympics and won their first Olympic gold.

Time was so short in the first competition, even though they were allowed to go last, that Anne only had ten minutes to warm up Dutch Bid. She stayed remarkably cool and focussed despite the incredible pressure and produced the best test that Cassidy had ever performed. Amazingly, they finished fourth individually – and the word quickly went round. Next day, everyone turned out to watch, including the whole of the German team and their trainers. Jennie and Desi were on tenterhooks as Anne came into the arena to start her test – and then, to their horror, there was a squeal of brakes and tyres from the road outside. Again, neither Anne nor Cassidy turned a hair and turned in a remarkable test.

At the end of the competition, Anne was sixth individually and the British team had won the silver medal. Jennie was as pleased and proud as if she had ridden to victory herself – as she announced, she had bred the horse and the rider! The reaction at home was amazing and not only gave a real boost to British dressage but gave it a whole new image in the eyes of young riders. Suddenly it was no longer second best to show jumping and eventing, but had acquired a new glamour. At one time, Desi was getting so many letters from mothers saying 'My daughter is interested in dressage, where do we start?' that she had to bring in three temporary secretaries to the Masterlock offices to cope with correspondence. With typical thoroughness and enthusiasm, she

The final piaffe on the centre line at the 1988 Olympics. Dutch Gold gave of his best and achieved an excellent fourteenth place (*Kit Houghton*)

Above: Dutch Gold wearing the Hermes rug. Dutch Gold also modelled the Hermes dressage saddle which Jennie helped to design (*Kit Houghton*)

Below: Aged twenty-three, Dutch Gold in the long reins in the parade at Burghley Horse Trials

Dazzler – son of Dutch Courage and on whom Jennie won the National Championships in 1995 for the last time before her retirement from competition (*Kit Houghton*)

Opposite page:
Catherston Dutch
Bid whom Jennie
describes as 'a
wonderful horse who
taught so many and
took four people to
international success'
(*Kit Houghton*)

Right: Desi Dillingham
on a tour of
Stockholm with
Jennie and David
Trott. Desi has been
a great supporter of
Catherston over many
years and is chairman
of British Dressage

Below: Stallion
viewing day at
Hurstbourne Priors

HRH The Princess Royal presents a British Horse Society award to Jennie
for services to equestrian training, 1998

Above: Lizzie after winning all three classes in the pouring rain at Hickstead on Catherston Humbug in 1999

Below: Jennie's grandchildren Christopher and Charlotte with their parents Anne and Brian Dicker (*Anthony Loriston-Clarke*)

Above: Dutch Courage – the founder of a dynasty (*Kit Houghton*)...

Below: Some of his descendants performing the quadrille at Hickstead 1999. (*left to right*) Lizzie on Catherston Humbug, Helen Williamson on Catherston Decipher, Jennie on Catherston Dazzler and Jodie Lister on Dutch Gold

made sure that every letter received a personal answer.

The Catherston team was not alone in prophesying a golden future for Cassidy, who went on to win a record number of international Prix St Georges competitions on British teams. Many others felt the same, and on one occasion Jennie turned down an open cheque. Sadly, Cassidy's star burned bright and then burned out. As his training progressed to the highest levels and Jennie rode him in competition, he showed that whilst his movement was fantastic, he just could not cope with the collection needed for piaffe. He started to show signs of lameness and stiffness but although everything was done to try and find out the cause, including expensive bone scans, it remained a mystery. Poor Cassidy would come out of the stable looking like an old, stiff horse, when in fact he should have been in his prime, and gradually become looser in his movement – but he was not capable of competing and it was not fair to make him work.

The big question was – what on earth could Jennie and Desi do with him? The answer was very little, because without knowing the cause of his problems there was little that could be done to put them right. The only thing that could be done – besides putting him down, which no one wanted to do – was to keep him comfortable on bute.

When Cassidy suffered a fluke bout of colic, abdominal pain that can lead to fatal complications, it seemed that the odds were piling up against him. Yet, ironically, this was to give him a new lease of life. He had to be operated on and when he came home, was only allowed to be led out in hand at walk. He got better and better and was soon feeling and looking so well that the vet told Jennie that they could start doing a bit more with him.

Watching the big horse stride out on his leadrope one morning, Jennie decided that it was time to see if Cassidy could get a little more out of life. Outwardly casual, but inwardly not sure what was going to happen, she suggested to Lizzie that she just get on him. After they had walked round with no ill effects, Jennie asked her to try a little trot and canter.

Both Cassidy and his rider were soon enjoying themselves, and to Jennie's pleasure they made a lovely combination. After consulting with

Desi, Jennie decided that although Cassidy would never be a Grand Prix horse, he could and should be a Young Riders mount. He therefore came back into competitive life with Lizzie, who also went into senior classes with him. Jennie never rode Cassidy in competition again, though she remained very fond of him and sometimes used him in lecture demonstrations.

Cassidy, who could play to the gallery only too well, loved an audience. At one lecture demo in which top riders demonstrated their training methods, Jennie joined forces with show jumper William Funnell. William had brought both novice and Grade A show jumpers to explain how he schooled them at different stages of their careers and at the end of their respective slots, they decided to swap disciplines.

Jennie started by putting William on Cassidy and teaching him to ride a few steps of passage and piaffe – because whilst the horse could not perform these to a sufficient level for serious competition, he could easily make an adequate attempt. William entered into the spirit of the occasion and so did Cassidy: the only difficulty William had was persuading him to stop passaging down the long side of the arena!

Then it was Jennie's turn for some fun. It was also time for the audience to be amazed, especially those who thought of her purely in terms of dressage. Riding one of William's horses, who soon went beautifully for her, she tackled progressively bigger fences until eventually the top rail was at a height that even a Grade A show jumper had serious respect for. The audience loved it and the cheers as she soared through the air were a recognition of her sense of fun as well as her ability. The lady who was heard to comment that never again would she think that all dressage riders were wimps probably spoke for many others in the audience that night.

Cassidy never suffered colic again and only retired fully at the age of nineteen. Sadly, he never really enjoyed retirement: most horses love being out in a field if they have company and shelter, but Cassidy was the exception. He would go out for an hour, eat grass and then decide he wanted to come in again. Age and stiffness caught up with him and he was put down at home at the age of twenty.

12

Like Father, Like Son

Whilst Dutch Courage was at the peak of his career, his son, Dutch Gold, was giving notice that he was also going to be a star. He showed such athleticism and jumping ability that he could have been as successful in eventing as he was in dressage; because he is three quarters Thoroughbred, he has the necessary speed and his offspring have excelled in both spheres.

After winning his second event, he gave Jennie another fabulous ride at Taunton Horse Trials. His winning streak continued at Brockenhurst, the local event, where he qualified for the Midland Bank Horse Trials Championships. Brockenhurst was a real family affair, with Anthony co-opted as a fence judge and Jane amongst the competitors. Jane's cross-country round was one that caused plenty of amusement afterwards, though she did not appreciate it at the time.

Anthony was judging at the next fence along and Jennie joined him to watch Jane's round. Unfortunately, Jane's horse hit the first part of the coffin complex and pinged her into the ditch that made up the second element. Her sister and brother-in-law rushed over to make sure that she was all right, joined by their local GP – the aptly named Dr Horsfall. Jane, who had been winded, opened her eyes and uttered the classic line, 'Where am I?' Jennie was able to inform her, with absolute accuracy, that she was lying in the coffin.

Next stop in Jennie and Willow's itinerary was Sherborne, where the course included a difficult double of corners. These are amongst the most difficult cross-country fences, because the rider has to get a precise line and be sure that the horse will not run out to the side; Jennie walked the course and decided that Willow would sail over the shorter, more difficult route.

To her surprise and mortification, the corners challenge was more than the still relatively inexperienced Willow could manage, and he ducked out. Rather than risk his confidence by attempting the same route again, she went for the alternative, easier one. Willow managed it easily, but Jennie was eliminated because she crossed her tracks and therefore gave herself a technical refusal. It was a salutary lesson and she never again set off on a course without a back-up plan for what she would do if anything went wrong at a particular fence.

With this in mind, Jennie took Willow to his next event with a definite game plan in mind. The course included a log into water, and although Willow was by now happy jumping in to and out of water, he could be very extravagant in his jumping style. She decided that the best approach was to come in slowly, but to ride positively so that he knew he must keep going forwards.

The positive approach became gradually more positive. Willow started off in trot, but ended up pinging into the water and as he leapt out, the drag of the water took effect and Jennie and he parted company. She emerged from her wet landing to see him trotting off away from the jump. The idea of a loose stallion with acres of cross-country course on which to amuse himself was unthinkable, and in desperation she called out, 'Willow, come here!'

If she needed any proof that she was establishing a bond with Willow, just as she had with his father, it was given to her in the next few seconds when he turned round and trotted back to her as obediently as a dog. In the midst of her relief, Jennie had time to be amused by a comment from the jump judge. 'Now that's what I call dressage,' the woman said admiringly.

Although Jennie had come off at a relatively low speed, she fell awkwardly and hurt her knee badly enough to make riding at their next planned event, Dauntsey, impossible. This caused for a rethink in tactics, because there was no way she wanted to head for the championships on a horse whose last cross-country experience involved a mishap at water. Anne's cool nerve supplied the answer, and with Mr Bannocks' permission she took over even though she had never ridden Willow before.

With no time to establish a relationship, their dressage test had to be something of a compromise. Anne found Willow very sensitive and although they were not always quite in tune with each other, they got to the end of the test without any major hiccoughs. This phase proved to be their biggest ordeal, and after a clear show jumping round they flew round the cross-country. Willow finished with his confidence completely restored and he and Jennie set off for the 1984 Midland Bank championships at Locko Park ready to take on everything the course designer could come up with.

The day could not have got off to a worst start. Anne, who was then eighteen and had passed her driving test, had qualified White Christmas and Pam Harvey Richards' lovely New Forest stallion, Deeracres Franco, for a regional dressage final. Mrs Harvey Richards lent her trailer and Anne set off early in the morning, unavoidably hitting the rush hour traffic in Southampton. Although no one knew quite what happened and she was driving very slowly, somehow she lost control — perhaps because either White Christmas or Franco became agitated by the hold-ups and started the trailer swaying from side to side. The momentum may have built up until Anne was unable to control the snaking trailer.

Minutes later, Jennie and Anthony got a phone call from the police to say that Anne had been involved in an accident. They rushed off in the horsebox to find that the trailer had flipped over and the Land Rover was facing the opposite way. Anne, not surprisingly, was sobbing with shock but was not hurt — and, miraculously, neither were the horses. They did not appear to have suffered even a scratch and walked calmly on to the horsebox as if nothing had happened. As a precaution, Jennie called the vet to check them over as soon as they got home, but apart from suggesting that they be kept in for a day or two in case of internal bruising, he found nothing wrong. Even their confidence remained untouched, and next time out both loaded and travelled as if nothing had happened.

Although Jennie's instinct was to stay at home with her daughter, Anne insisted that she would feel even worse if Willow did not take part in the championships. Once she was sure that Anne would be all right and the secretary at Catherston, Jenny Care, had promised to keep an eye on her, Jennie and Anthony set off for Locko Park with Jane, who had volunteered to go along as helper and confidence booster.

Sensibly, Jane suggested that they should go and see how the course's water jump was riding so that Jennie could plan her approach and route through it. Twelve horses later, only one had gone through clear and Jennie – who had been feeling apprehensive to start with – was left distinctly worried. Yet once she got on Dutch Gold her nerves melted away: he was as fit as he had ever been and by now, knew what was in store. In fact, he was probably fitter than he needed to be, as he was entered for Rotterdam Show, his first international appearance, the weekend after.

Although he was full of sparkle, his dressage test was controlled and accurate and he found the show jumping course easy. As they set off on the cross-country Jennie found that she was actually enjoying herself;

Willow certainly was. Because he was due to leave for Rotterdam on the next day, she aimed to cruise round rather than risk tiring the horse, but Willow was so fit and found it all so easy that they arrived at the dreaded water complex full of running. Jennie sat tight, clicked her tongue to encourage him and he went through as if he was splashing through a puddle on a forest ride.

Ironically, their only precarious moment came at the next fence, a double built across a road. Perhaps because she was so relieved to have come through the water so easily, Jennie lost concentration for a moment and they came in on a bad stride. Willow made the first element but was totally wrong for the second, a fruit barrow. There was no way he could clear it, but he was coming in on such a slow approach he managed to bank it, jumping on a beautifully arranged collection of melons as he did so. Jennie's impression was of a minor mid-air glitch, but the gasps from spectators at the fence revealed that it looked much more dramatic than it felt.

It also left Dutch Gold the winner of the Midland Bank Horse Trials Championship. If he had gone on with his eventing career, he could have been a Badminton horse, but he had such an abundance of talent that Jennie soon realised that she had her next Grand Prix horse – he actually competed in his first Grand Prix tests in 1985.

Willow's first appearance in an international dressage arena did not immediately signal that here was a future star, but even though they finished halfway down the field, Jennie was not worried. The stallion had travelled well and concentrated as much as she could expect on his job, which probably seemed much less exciting to him than flying round the cross-country at Locko Park. She went home knowing that they had a lot to work on, but quietly confident that the talent and the temperament were there for her to work with.

From the start, Willow was a sensitive, vivacious horse who combined power with elegance. The more he did, the more confident he grew and as an eight-year-old showed clear signs that he was a horse to be reckoned with in the dressage arena. He and Jennie travelled to Aachen, where he was the only horse who was warmed up for the Prix St Georges classes over show jumps!

It sounds unorthodox, but Jennie knew her horse and knew that she had to keep his active mind occupied. Willow has always revelled in doing different things and she decided that taking him into the show jumpers' warm-up area and working over small fences was the best way of preparing him mentally and physically. The results showed that once again, her lateral thinking had paid off, because Willow was well placed and riders on the international circuit were starting to notice that this son of the great Dutch Courage had plenty to offer on his own account.

Then, unbelievably, it seemed that Jennie might lose him. The recession hit many British businesses, including Donald Bannocks' — and though he did not want to, he was forced into deciding that he would have to sell Dutch Gold. Realising what it would mean to Jennie to lose the ride, Mr Bannocks gave her a month to try and find a buyer or team of buyers. Jennie knew how generous he was being, because a rich Italian already had his eye on Willow and she suspected that he may already have made an offer.

Desi Dillingham was equally determined that Dutch Gold should carry no other flag than the Union Jack and no other rider than Jennie. Through her incredible network of contacts she came up with Margaret Clayton, a clever and resourceful woman who lived and worked in London and had a great interest in dressage. She agreed to take a share in Willow and became part owner with Jennie and Anthony. Jennie acknowledges that Mr Bannocks did all he could to help, as he could probably have got a bigger price from abroad, and has always felt sorry that he did not have the thrill of owning him when he went on that year to do so well.

However, Margaret Clayton soon became a friend as well as a financial saviour. Now retired, she comes to see Willow whenever possible and has great affection for him as a character as well as admiration for him as an athlete. Over the years she has combined her enthusiasm for dressage with an enjoyment of travel, and has frequently watched him competing abroad and then broadened her horizons still farther — in Seoul, she went from the spectator seats round the dressage arena to exploring its remotest areas.

Dutch Courage's retirement in 1985 was a serious blow for British dressage, as there were very few horses competing at that level. Dutch Gold had to quickly step out from being the understudy into playing a leading role, and at nine years old was in the British team at Copenhagen. He had reached Grand Prix level remarkably quickly and soon showed that he had an exceptional talent for dressage to music – a relatively new idea which was to make the sport more attractive and entertaining to those outside its specialist confines.

Today, dressage has a glamour and cachet undreamt of in the 1980s. In Holland, Anky van Grunsven has the status and following of a chart-topping singer or fashion model, complete with official fan club and her own range of clothing. In Britain, the teenagers whose parents perhaps dreamed of becoming the next Lucinda Green or Ian Stark are just as likely to dream of emulating the success of Carl Hester or Lizzie. Dressage is no longer something to do if you can't jump – it has become a desirable goal in its own right.

The acceptance at international level of freestyle dressage to music was the beginning of the sport's rise to widespread popularity. Its enter-tainment value blossomed and for the first time, dressage became a true spectator sport, appealing not only to those who appreciated the technical elements, but to anyone who took pleasure from the sight of horse and rider in harmony, their performance enhanced by music. For the riders, there was the added challenge and fascination of devising a routine which incorporated compulsory movements and choosing music which complemented their horses.

Jennie had always had a natural feel for music and now she was in her element. So was Willow, because his lightness and elegance came to the fore; his early performances were performed to English, Scottish and Irish reels and the judges and spectators loved the dancing stallion.

Today, top level dressage to music is high powered and choreo-graphing routines and setting music is a skill in itself. Then, it was a very Heath Robinson affair – Jennie would ride through the test whilst Anthony filmed it, and they would then work through their library of records, recording and splicing tapes. Opinions varied and there were times when discussions became decidedly heated. Sometimes, they would put together music which seemed just right in theory, but when Jennie rode the test she would find problems.

Jennie jokes that devising Dutch Gold's music brought her and Anthony the closest they have ever come to divorce. Fortunately, Claire Morrison, one of their students, had a great knowledge and appreciation of music and became Jennie's 'musical director'. Claire, now a successful rider and trainer, had her own recording equipment and a vast musical library, so Willow's repertoire extended dramatically. Anthony discovered some equipment which enabled him to speed up or slow down the music to suit Willow's way of going perfectly, and harmony was restored on all levels.

Audiences soon came to appreciate Jennie's performances, particularly when she was able to ride to music that held a special appeal. In Gothenburg, she was given an enthusiastic reception when she and Willow performed to the Swedish Rhapsody, including a sequence where she rode canter zigzags with the reins in one hand, and in Paris, their performance included a piece called 'The Poor People of Paris'.

As Willow's career began to take off, Jennie decided that, tactically, she needed to get wider acceptance of his ability from the judges. The best way to do this, she felt, was to go to every major indoor show it was possible to get to and thus exploit his talent for dressage to music. Her tactics were dramatically successful and – just for starters – they won World Cup qualifiers in Holland and Brussels.

Jennie was not the only member of the family scoring competition successes. Both her daughters were doing well, Lizzie having decided to specialise in dressage but Anne attracted above all to the challenge of eventing. Anne was one of those rare riders with a natural gift; she could get on any horse and instinctively work out what made it tick and how to get the best out of it. This, coupled with her enthusiasm and boldness, meant that she had all the promise to get right to the top of the eventing world.

The horse on which she started her eventing career was far from easy: Wellingtonia, a big, talented mare with an attitude to match. Originally, Wellie came to Catherston for a serious sort out, as she had learned that if she did not want to go somewhere, whipping round and standing on her back legs was enough to make most riders back down from a confrontation. She quickly found that in Anne, she had met her match, but the mare's stroppiness was gradually turned into an enthusiasm for work and particularly cross-country.

Wellie was returned to her owner, but as so often happens, reverted to her previous bad behaviour when she realised she could get away with it. She was sent back to Catherston to be sold, but although she behaved perfectly when Anne rode her, she still tried it on with any new rider. Whenever anyone came to see her, she went well in the school and was equally obedient in the field. The potential buyer would then ask to ride her down the road, and a few minutes later would return, Wellie having succeeded in suggesting it was time to go home. She was not a saleable proposition, and in the end Donald Bannocks offered to buy her as a gift for Anne to event. Their eventing career got off to a great start, and Wellie and Anne scorched through junior competitions and were equally successful as they graduated to novice and intermediate.

In 1987, Anne's hopes were shattered by a road accident. Unbelievably, it was the second time she was the victim of an uninsured driver. The first accident was in the summer of 1984, when a reckless teenager, showing off in a car that he had swapped for a motor bike only that morning, lost control on a newly surfaced road and ploughed into Anne's car, leaving her with back and shoulder injuries.

Two years later and just three weeks before Christmas, she was again a blameless victim. This time, the driver had just bought a new car but had not told his insurance company. The results of Anne's injuries were devastating – the bones in one foot were shattered and her knee was broken straight across. She was rushed to hospital and straight to the operating theatre; afterwards, the surgeon told her that she would probably never walk properly again and that her riding career was over.

It was an appalling blow, for Anne and her family. At first, none of them could believe that her ambitions and career had been ended in such a way – but although she was very depressed at first, Anne knew that she had to not only pick up her life again, but steer a different course. The opportunity to do that came via a phone call from the late

Raymond Brooks-Ward, whose voice was familiar to millions of television viewers as the nation's favourite show jumping commentator.

Raymond asked Anne if she would like a job as secretary for the Royal International Horse Show, which meant she would be a member of the organising team. She had no secretarial experience and had never been involved in show organisation, but it was too good an offer to turn down. In any case, she had been brought up to believe that whatever job you did, you did it properly – so took the chance in both hands.

Anne started her job after the May Bank Holiday and the show was scheduled for 11 June . There was no time to be nervous, only to surface from being thrown in at the deep end and start swimming. The practicalities of it came naturally to her and soon she was not only coping with the job, but enjoying it. It meant long hours, but as Anne was a natural night bird that did not worry her – the only problem came when she was walking through London's diplomatic square in the early hours of one morning after leaving the show offices. It took all her powers of persuasion to persuade a suspicious policeman that she was an honest worker returning home, rather than a spy.

Later, the experience gained during her years with the Royal International and Horse of the Year Show paid dividends when she helped to start off Catherston's shows and organisation, a role she will be carrying out for the new owners. She has always enjoyed teaching and has remained involved with the practical side, too. Even better, over the past year she has made a cautious return to riding. It is still too early to know if she will be able to compete again and she will certainly not be able to event, but after being told that she would never ride again, anything is a bonus – particularly as she has a lovely five-year-old mare out of Wellingtonia, by Dutch Gold, to bring on.

As the family began to adjust, Jennie had the 1988 Seoul Olympics in sight. Her record with Dutch Gold meant that when the selectors came to pick the British team, they were certainties for a place. Fate and politics had denied Dutch Courage his chance at Olympic glory, but his son could not be ignored. Willow now faced the longest flight of his career, though Jennie at least had the comfort of knowing that her brother Mike and his team were in charge of the arrangements.

In fact, the only part of the journey he did not like was when the travelling crate was loaded on to the aircraft by forklift. As he was lifted up and placed down again, Willow showed his disapproval by performing piaffe. The riders, too, had their own moments of discomfort to put up with: the long flight necessitated a stop-off in Moscow for re-fuelling, but a group of Russian soldiers – puny youths with spotty faces and machine guns – made it clear that they were not to leave the plane.

Unfortunately, freestyle to music was not part of the Olympic competition: it was not until the Sydney Olympics in 1992 that it was to be brought in at this level. Despite that, Jennie at least had the satisfaction that Willow's performance was by far the best of the British, leaving them in fourteenth place individually.

It may seem strange that a horse could compete in an Olympic Games before he was at the peak of his ability, but the partnership of Jennie and Dutch Gold was still improving. Two years later saw them finish thirteenth in the World Championships and they then started on a winning roll that gained spectacular momentum. Between 1988 and 1990 the stallion won six World Cup qualifiers, the only British horse ever to have achieved such a record, and took two fourth and two fifth places in World Cup finals. In every case, it was superb tests to music that boosted their final placings.

Dutch Gold's strengths were his lightness and athleticism, coupled with sheer joy of living. Ironically, the courage and boldness and the impatience with inactivity that made him such a star in the eventing field during his early years perhaps showed as his only weak link in pure dressage. He could and did perform all the advanced movements with panache, but the one thing he found difficult – mentally, rather than physically – was movements in walk. Jennie says that his walk was always too busy and he would not let himself relax into the pace – mainly because walking was boring and he would far rather be doing something more exciting.

However, although he would not be in the top half dozen after the Grand Prix, as soon as his music began he and Jennie showed the others how it should be done. Their greatest musical achievement of all came in Berlin, just after the Wall came down in 1989, thanks to Jennie's cool nerve and the remarkable rapport she had built up with her horse. If ever she needed proof that Dutch Gold was a worthy successor to his sire, this was it.

Anyone running a book on the competition would have marked them down as outsiders. A good but not quite good enough Grand Prix test left them in fifth place and Jennie knew that she was going to have to pull out all the stops to overtake the riders ahead of her – particularly Isabelle Werth, a clear favourite on home ground with Weingart.

She rode into the arena totally focussed, knowing that this was no time for half measures. Dutch Gold, too, seemed to know that this occasion demanded brilliance and co-operation and responded brilliantly as Jennie asked what many riders would never have dared to. With the reins in one hand, she fired the full power of the horse's extension, then contained that energy in collection, harnessing the power without Dutch Gold showing any signs of resentment. The murmurs started to build around the crowd, exploding into gasps of amazement and smatterings of applause as – with Jennie still holding the reins in one hand – they danced their way through the canter zig-zags.

Their programme was incredibly difficult, but the knowledgeable crowd appreciated both the technical perfection and the artistry. So did the judges: their final score was more than seventy per cent, which in those days was a rare achievement and the highest Jennie had ever achieved.

She rode out of the arena knowing that she and Dutch Gold had done their absolute best. All she could do now was wait and see whether Isabelle could do better. As the German rider began her programme, it was obvious that she had been watching Jennie and was not going to concede the place on the winner's rostrum without a fight. Good though her performance was, she was riding a big, powerful horse and could not match Dutch Gold for lightness and expression.

At the press conference afterwards, one of the journalists asked Jennie if riding with the reins in one hand was truly classical. Quick off the mark, she replied that if the leader of the Spanish Riding School could do it, so could she. Colonel Alois Podjhasky performed the whole of the

Pas Seul, the individual display, with the reins in one hand and Jennie's reckoning was that you could not get more classical than that.

In Germany, Jennie was a star, even if her fame was mainly that she had beaten Isabelle, the favourite, on her home ground. If a homebred horse had won there or in Holland, the horse world – and not just the dressage specialists – would have gone wild at such an achievement. At home in Britain, the reaction was depressingly familiar and there was barely a ripple of interest.

And whilst her horse's performance was reward enough in itself, Jennie cannot help a rueful smile as she compares the prizes that were awarded then with those of later years. She won a whip: if she had ridden to victory ten years later, she would have been able to drive off in a new car.

13

Catherston
Moves On

The early 1990s saw Catherston's breeding policy producing exciting and talented results, both for the Loriston-Clarkes and for other breeders. In 1985 Jennie and Tessa Clarke, then her head girl, became pioneers of the use of artificial insemination in breeding competition horses. Now, it is used worldwide and many competing stallions are only available by this method; then, it was breaking new ground.

Jennie and Tessa – who first came to Catherston for three weeks to help with Jane's event horses and stayed for eleven years – met Professor Twink Allen, one of the leading authorities in the field, and learned all they could from him about the use of AI. Jennie knew that if she could introduce it for Catherston, it would be the ideal way of expanding the business. Dutch Courage was much sought after, but limited acreage plus his competition commitments meant that it was impractical to take in a lot of visiting mares.

Jennie started by running a pilot scheme, using mares owned by the Gilbey family on the Isle of Man. This worked so well that Catherston began using AI commercially, with excellent results. For the first time, breeders impressed by the stock Dutch Courage was producing and eager to use him on their own mares were not limited by distance.

Catherston Dazzler had caught the eye of many when he made his first public appearance as a yearling at his sire's 'retirement party' at

Goodwood in 1985; his dam was Welton Gazelle, bred by Sam Barr at his Welton Stud, the home of so many top event horses. Gazelle, an advanced eventer, was loaned to Catherston by her owners, the Johnsons, because she was difficult to get in foal – but she could not resist Bill.

Dazzler, like Dutch Courage, could do anything. He won the Masterlock Potential Competition Horse finals in 1988 and 1989 and in the same years was also awarded the *Horse & Hound* prize for the best potential show jumper. Olympic show jumper Malcolm Pyrah, one of the judges, rode him and said afterwards that the stallion had so much scope over a fence, he felt he was never going to come back to earth. Dazzler could have been equally successful eventing, and showed his versatility in 1990 by winning the Stora Timber open dressage and jumping championships, but was destined for an international dressage career. This started when he won the British novice championship with Jennie.

At the same time, a lovely colt called Catherston Dance in the Dark was enjoying the free and easy life of a yearling. By Bill out of Catherston Lonely Breeze – a daughter of Desert Storm and Xenocles – he soon showed that he had both presence and character and in later years, when his turn came to stand at stud, one of his favourite tricks was to stick out his tongue at visitors.

The 1990 crop of foals included two spectacular colts who were to become equally spectacular stallions and dressage horses. Catherston Humbug is by Liboi, a versatile Thoroughbred who won ten races and was placed twenty-three times on the Flat and over hurdles from seventy-one starts. When he retired from racing, Liboi's owner, Margaret Blackburn, felt that he deserved a special home.

She and the horse's trainer, Rosemary Lomax, came to one of Catherston's stallion viewing days and were convinced that this environment would be ideal for him. Jennie agreed to stand him at the stud and he soon proved to be equally talented off the racecourse. Proof of his superb temperament came in 1983, when he was supreme champion at the Ponies of Britain show, both in-hand and under saddle, ridden by the then thirteen-year-old Lizzie. Liboi had a long and happy life and was finally put down at the age of twenty-seven.

Catherston Decipher, another of Bill's sons, is out of Choiseul Sound. Her sire, Roedean Rhythm N'Blues, is by the Arab stallion Donax. Decipher is yet another Catherston stallion to become a successful advanced dressage horse. He has fifteen per cent Arab blood and its traces can be seen in his beautiful head and natural carriage, which he passes on to his children. Jennie also loves him for his fantastic, trainable temperament: she finds that some part-bred Arabs have a 'Don't push me or I'll push you back' attitude, but Decipher has never had a mean thought in his life.

Every year, Dutch Courage's influence grew stronger. In 1991, Catherston Lonely Breeze gave birth to his grandson, Catherston Gold Storm – by Dutch Gold. This future stallion and dressage horse was to be the last of her children and, sadly, the beginning of his life was followed later that year by the end of Dutch Courage's. In November of that year Bill suddenly became ill and on 13 November Jennie had to take the terrible decision to have him put down.

Until his last illness, Bill was in top condition and still proving that he could be a superb showman: just a month before, Jennie had used him in a demonstration of long reining, which both he and the audience enjoyed. Jennie had become well-known for her skills in long reining, where the horse is controlled and directed from the ground. It is both an art and a skill demanding sensitivity, timing and quick reactions on the part of the handler and Jennie is one of the few people who can teach advanced movements such as half pass and passage on the long reins.

As soon as Bill showed the first signs of distress by breaking out in a sweat, Jennie called the vet, recognising that the stallion had colic – though what she could not tell at that stage was that he had a gangrenous gut. He went rapidly downhill and accepting that he was too ill to operate on, she took what she knew was the only decision. Dutch Courage was put down at home at the age of twenty-two. He was irreplaceable, but left a far-reaching legacy – his children, grandchildren and great-grandchildren are the greatest memorial he could have.

His last foals, including Catherston Dynasty and Catherston Demoiselle, were born in 1992. Dynasty later had to be put down after injuring his back, but Demoiselle went on to a successful eventing career and was later an equally successful broodmare. She was out of May Dancer, the last horse owned by Miss Profumo and left to Jennie in the latter's will.

Catherston would never be the same without Dutch Courage, but Jennie knew that by continuing Dutch Gold's successful career she was keeping Bill's name alive. The Barcelona Olympics were only a year away and in most people's judgement, Willow was a certainty for a team place. His record was outstanding, he was performing at his peak and Jennie had unparalleled experience of competing at Olympic level. In a team situation, this sort of background is invaluable, because although every competition is different, a rider who understands the stresses and demands can boost the confidence of less experienced members and help them get the maximum out of themselves and their horses.

After horses on the shortlist were assessed, Jennie was told that she and Dutch Courage were not on the team. At that time, Diana Mason, who had so generously lent her own horse, Prince Consort, to Jennie when Dutch Courage was unable to travel to Los Angeles, was chairman of the then British Dressage Group, chief of the selectors and chef d'equipe to the British team. She told Jennie that Willow had shown signs of slight unlevelness in trot – and whilst Jennie appreciated that there could be no question marks over an Olympic contender's sound-ness, she was sure that the stallion was one hundred per cent. To make absolutely sure, she called the team vet, John McEwan, who told her that he had not seen any sign of a problem.

The original decision stayed, though it was one which caused a lot of controversy: Dutch Gold did not go to the Olympics. Instead, Jennie rode him on the British team in Rotterdam, where he finished third in the first class. The prize giving was held in the main arena, which had become boggy, and Willow decided it was all too exciting. Jennie managed to contain him but he had worked up such a sweat she had to ride him in walk to cool him off.

When he had settled, she took him back to the stables to wash him down. Ten minutes later, she came back to check him and found Willow throwing his head about in agitation. Jennie asked him to take a step forwards and found, to her horror, that he was hopping around on three legs.

Because there was no sign of heat or swelling, she knew that the problem must be sited in Willow's foot. A Dutch vet thought it was a case of poison in the foot – a build-up of infection inside, perhaps caused by a puncture wound – and cut holes in Willow's hoof to try and find the site. A poultice was put on to try and draw out any infection, but Willow was in such pain that Jennie knew there was no hope of him competing in any other classes.

Next day, he was no better and the Dutch vet told her that he thought he had broken his pedal bone. Jennie could not believe this and was so worried by his initial treatment of the stallion that she did not want him to be in charge of farther investigations. The King's Troop Royal Horse Artillery team was performing its display at the show, and she asked them to give her some bute so that she could at least relieve Willow's pain.

As soon as it took effect and he was fit to travel, she loaded him on to the lorry and brought him home. As soon as they arrived, Jennie's own vet took over. She found, to her surprise but also relief, that poison in the foot was, after all, the root of the problem. It was so deep inside the structures of the hoof that the pressure of the pus trying to come out had probably been building up for several days – but Willow was

so tough that he only went lame at crisis point.

Ironically, this was the first and only occasion on which he was ever lame and Jennie remains adamant that until after his excellent performance in the first class at Rotterdam, he had showed no signs of lameness. She retired him from competition later that year, aged sixteen. Jennie made the decision not through sour grapes but because she wanted Willow to go out at the top, in a year when he had come fifth in the Volvo World Cup finals. He had given his all, had nothing left to prove and she did not want him to remain competing and be beaten by younger horses when age gradually started to take its toll.

Although being left off the team for the Barcelona Olympics was a blow, Jennie refused to do anything but think positive. She jokes that she and Anthony decided that if the Olympics were off their personal agenda, they would move house, instead. Anthony had recently retired but even if he had wanted it, a leisurely retirement was the last thing that lay ahead.

Catherston was bursting at the seams. It had more top class stallions standing than probably any other stud in the UK, with others waiting in the wings, plus mares and youngstock. It was impossible to find anywhere in the New Forest with enough land, but when Anthony's mother decided to move into a home in Brockenhurst, Black Knoll went on the market and Jennie and Anthony started searching for a new base in Hampshire.

Pear Tree Farm had already been sold, which reduced their grazing land to twenty-two acres – which with twenty-eight horses, was bordering on the desperate. They spent many hours searching for the right place, then through an agent heard that a former dairy farm at Hurstbourne Priors, near Whitchurch, might be coming up for sale. Manor Farm was potentially ideal; the land ranged from water meadows with a river running through to hills on chalkland, with a lovely manor house. In a perfect setting, but with easy access to major roads, it offered enormous possibilities.

Negotiations started, and the final haggling was carried out over the telephone from a Gothenburg hotel, as Jennie was competing abroad. The sale was agreed and in August 1992 horses, people and equipment moved home. It was an exercise in logistics that few would care to make

– the last doors were actually being put on the stables as the horses arrived – but thanks to help from family and friends, they made it. However, there was no time to relax, because the real work on the land had to start immediately. The previous owners had become so fed up with trying to meet European regulations that they had ploughed up much of the 350 acres and turned it over to corn. That left Jennie and Anthony with sixty acres of grazing, but the rest had to be put down to grazing and fenced.

Over the next few years, a continual programme of expansion and improvements turned Catherston Stud into what was once described as one of the jewels of the British horse world. It became not only one of – if not the – leading centres in the UK for the breeding and training of competition horses, but also one of the top educational establishments and show centres. Yet in a peculiar Catch 22 situation, the superb facilities that made it so successful also made it a huge burden for Jennie and Anthony.

It was essential to build an indoor school and they were advised that because they were an educational establishment and the building could also be used for non-equestrian purposes, government funding would be available. Building went ahead on the £250,000 project only for them to discover that the grant which they thought had been awarded no longer existed, because the then Sports Council had changed its identity. Running shows and hiring out the facilities were no longer a useful option, they were essential for Catherston's existence.

At its busiest, any week could see it being used as a venue for everything from top level dressage and show jumping competitions to dog agility and clear round jumping. Students came from all over the world and to be able to say that you had trained at Catherston under Jennie Loriston-Clarke was the horse world's equivalent of an Oxbridge education.

Jennie also used the centre's facilities to try and improve the welfare of animals on the New Forest. When they first moved there, she was appalled at some of the treatment she saw meted out, most of it caused by ignorance and all of it accepted as normal practice. Pony owners would put halters on their foals and expect them to lead, resorting to force when – not surprisingly – the foals became frightened and resisted. Brute strength was the accepted way of doing things.

Worst of all was the case of a pretty little New Forest mare who she had first seen as a two-year-old, and whose owner booked her in the following year to be covered by one of the stallions. The mare arrived whilst Jennie was out and when she returned she discovered, to her horror, that the pony's headcollar was embedded in its flesh. It had not been removed or adjusted since it was put on the year before and as the pony grew, became first tight and eventually embedded in its head. Jennie managed to cut it off and treat the pony before calling her owner and telling him what she thought of him.

Realising that the only way to combat ignorance was through education, she organised lecture demonstrations for local owners and riding clubs on all aspects of horse care and management, from educating youngsters to the importance of good farriery. By getting the message across to younger riders, she helped to ensure that the younger generation, at least, saw their ponies and their own responsibilities in a new light.

Catherston's stallion viewing days became one of the highlights of the equestrian year. Originally devised so that prospective breeders could not only see the stallions perform under saddle but also view their youngstock, they became well-known for their entertainment value. Where else could you see the unique combination of the country's top dressage stallions, followed by a 'show jumping performance' by Jennie's lurcher, Harry?

Jennie was one of the few breeders to realise that producing good horses was not enough to guarantee a market for them. The stallion days were a way of showing what Catherston had to offer, but she was also conscious of the fact that British breeders needed a way to show off their horses and hopefully get a return on their investment. She was determined to find a way to boost the industry – and, helped by Paul Fielder, came up with the idea of the High Performance Sales.

The idea was simple, but effective. Breeders and owners, whether they ran large studs or had a single nice animal, were invited to bring top quality foals to five-year-olds for assessment at specially organised days throughout the country. A panel of experienced and knowledgeable selectors made sure that those accepted for the sale had the conformation, movement and athleticism to promise a competitive future; later, as the running of the sale was refined, entrants were also pre-vetted.

Ridden horses were brought to the Royal Agricultural Centre at Stoneleigh, Warwickshire, two weeks before the auction. Here they were ridden and prepared by a team of expert riders, under Jennie's supervision, to ensure that they were happy in their surroundings and could be shown off to their best advantage. Viewing days were arranged so that prospective buyers could see the horses in the stables and being worked, so that when auction time came, they knew as much as possible about the horses they were bidding for.

The sale itself was turned into a spectacular occasion, with a gala evening and displays. At first, it was an incredible success: the highest price at the first sale was £20,000, which fifteen years ago was almost unheard of. Many horses sold through the High Performance Sales went on to make their mark at international level, including international event horses Primmore's Pride, Crown Feldspar, MJ's Fires Out and Market Venture.

Many of the top priced horses went abroad. Sadly and frustratingly, this was yet another sign that British riders are not prepared to invest in British-bred horses, and over the years the top sale prices went down rather than up. At the final one, the best price realised was a depressing £10,000, which meant that the sale was just not a viable proposition.

No one has been more serious about breeding and producing top class horses than Jennie and she finds it constantly frustrating that some riders are prepared to pay serious money for foreign-bred horses and ignore the fact that they could buy as good or better at home. Yet she has never lost her sheer pleasure in riding and her sense of fun, both qualities that have helped to make her such a good teacher.

Even when she was at the height of her own competitive career, she gained as much pleasure from seeing Anne and Lizzie making their names. Lizzie's name became more and more familiar and Jennie could see that if her youngest daughter was to achieve her potential, she needed the chance of top class rides – the horses she herself was riding. She also felt that it was unfair for Lizzie to be forever riding in her shadow and decided that there was only one answer.

After an international career spanning more than thirty years, Jennie announced that she was retiring from top level dressage. Lizzie took over the rides on Dazzler and Decipher and forged a tremendous partnership with Humbug, who she has brought on from the start. Together, they have a wide range of international successes and Jennie has never regretted hanging up her competitive top hat.

The decision to step back from top level competition gave her more time to develop other areas of her life, particularly international judging and teaching. She and Anthony were also able to look at their life, which made them realise that rather than them running Catherston, the empire that Catherston had become was running them.

Early in 2001, Manor Farm was sold. Jennie and Anthony decided that to go forward, they needed to streamline and to concentrate on breeding and producing competition horses. The name of Catherston Stud is now borne by Croft Farm, a quarter of an hour's car journey away. When Jennie and Anthony look through the window of their new dining room, they see the mares with this year's foals – the latest generation to bear the great bloodlines of Dutch Courage.

Lizzie, who married Will Murray in 1999 wearing the family heirloom wedding dress, continues to train and compete the Catherston stallions. Anne married Brian Dicker, an agricultural contractor, in 1996 and they have two children, four-year-old Christopher and three-year-old Charlotte. When her parents moved to Croft Farm, Anne stayed at Hurstbourne Priors to run a livery yard and competition centre at their old home for the new owners.

As soon as Jennie and Anthony moved in, the phone started ringing again. Whilst they were unpacking boxes, visitors were wanting to see young horses for sale and view the stallions – of whom Dutch Gold is still the boss. At twenty-five years old, he is still performing advanced movements on long reins, and covering mares. When Jennie goes to see him, he will still piaffe in his stable and then look at her as if to say, 'That's what you wanted me to do, isn't it?'

Soon the new house bore witness to her incredible career, from mementoes of early victories with Desert Storm and Kadett to triumphs with Dutch Courage and Dutch Gold. Amongst them is an award which came not from the world of dressage but which symbolises much wider recognition and appreciation.

During 2000, Jennie was persuaded to accompany her sister, Jane, to a fund-raising lunch at a London hotel. This was an annual event organised by the Animal Health Trust, one of Europe's leading veterinary and research centres; its centre for equine research has carried out vital work in a huge range of conditions, including strangles and equine viral arteritis and carried out groundbreaking research in the field of genetics.

One of its most notable achievements of recent years has been a research project led by Dr David Marlin into the effects of heat and humidity on horses. This was started before the 1996 Olympic Games, to make sure that horses would be able to cope with climatic conditions in Atlanta and then to define the best ways of looking after them. It was an area of research that affected all disciplines, including dressage, and which had far-reaching implications for horse welfare all over the world. Jane had booked a table and persuaded Jennie that not only was it a valuable cause but it would be a really fun occasion.

Jane was right, on both counts. At the end of the lunch, the trust made a series of awards to those who had achieved excellence in various areas of the horse world, from veterinary research to sporting achievement. Jennie was in the middle of an intense discussion with one of the winners, Vere Phillips – who won universal admiration when he came fourth at Burghley a year after his wife, Polly, was killed in a cross-country fall – when she heard her name.

Jennie had been so busy discussing with Vere, a dealer in top class horses, how important it was to pass on details of horses' breeding when they were sold that she had lost track of what was going on around them. Suddenly she realised that the details were being announced of another award… and that she was the recipient.

Jane, with the connivance of Jennie's secretary, Fiona Boyne, had managed to keep secret from her sister that this was no ordinary lunch. Jennie was presented with a 'lifetime achievement' award in recognition of her many accomplishments, as a rider, breeder and ambassador for the horse world. When she had time to recover from the shock, Jennie felt both moved and proud – and glad that Jane and Fiona had managed to keep the award secret so she did not need to worry about it beforehand.

Her huge range of experience as a breeder, trainer, rider and teacher means that since she officially retired from top class competition she has been in great demand as a judge; as one rider puts it, albeit rather ruefully, 'You can't get anything past her, but she's ready to be positive. You don't feel that she's sitting there in her little box waiting for you to screw up.'

Jennie's passport gains more and more stamps through international judging, though they are sometimes more interesting than glamorous. In 2001 a trip to a centre near Minsk, in Belarus, left her with two strong convictions. One was that riders and horses in Britain should count their blessings – and the other was that if she ever returned, the one essential item in her suitcase would be a loo seat. Throughout the three-day trip, she only saw one; somehow, it symbolised how Belarus lacked so much that so many other countries take for granted. She soon discovered that most places had running water, but whether anything happened or not when you turned on the taps was another matter; electricity supplies were similarly unpredictable

Jennie and her fellow judges were accompanied throughout their stay by an interpreter, a charming and intelligent young woman who had to work in two jobs – one in the daytime and another in the evenings – to be able to afford just a basic standard of living. As a judge, Jennie was paid the equivalent of £30 per day through the FEI, which is less than many British trainers charge for a single lesson. Because she was there to try and help and encourage the development of dressage, the financial side was not something she had considered, but she discovered that her token fee was the equivalent of two and a half months' salary for their interpreter.

At the centre, the competition horses looked well enough, but the more she looked behind the scenes, the more Jennie realised how difficult things were. Apart from the elite animals, the horses, who were mostly stallions, were thin to the point of emaciation. The more she found out about the way people existed in Belarus, the more she realised why.

They could not afford to worm their horses or to provide other routine medication that British and European owners take for granted. They could not even make hay in large enough quantities to store for later in the year, because they could not afford machinery. Jennie realised just what a different world it was when she saw grass being cut and taken to the horses in the stables by horse and cart. It was like stepping back in time, overlaid by an ugly taint of corruption. Cars were few and far between and the driver of that provided for the judges was careful to stay below the speed limits – but this did not prevent a policeman stopping them and trying to extort a 'fine' for speeding.

Her trip made her even more conscious of the importance of education and practical help to safeguard horse welfare. She returned home to find that she had been given another award in recognition of her lifetime commitment to just that: the Worshipful Company of Farriers, one of 102 livery companies in the City of London which carry on the heritage of the old craft guilds, had made her an honorary freeman. The history of this illustrious company dates back to 1356 and only a handful of people, including the Princess Royal, are currently recognised in this way.

Jennie appreciates both this and the Animal Health Trust Award for several reasons. One is that they have been made not just in recognition of her achievements as a competitor, trainer and breeder, but as acknowledgement of her commitment to raising standards in all aspects of horse care and welfare. She also looks on them as a tribute not just to her, but to her parents, who taught her so much. Last but not least, they have been shared by her horses. From Mossy the pony to the great stallions, Dutch Courage and his son, Dutch Gold, they have shaped her life and helped make her what she is today.

Not that the story is over yet. Jennie still has plenty of plans and ambitions – in particular, she hopes that one day, she will see Lizzie win an Olympic medal on a homebred horse. She has neither the inclination nor the temperament to rest on her laurels and even if she had, the phone at Catherston would not stop ringing for long enough to give her the chance.

Index

181

INDEX

INDEX

INDEX